Friedrich Ballhorn

Grammatography

A Manual of Reference to the Alphabets of Ancient and Modern

Languages

Friedrich Ballhorn

Grammatography
A Manual of Reference to the Alphabets of Ancient and Modern Languages

ISBN/EAN: 9783337090135

Printed in Europe, USA, Canada, Australia, Japan

Cover: Foto ©Thomas Meinert / pixelio.de

More available books at **www.hansebooks.com**

GRAMMATOGRAPHY

A

MANUAL OF REFERENCE

TO THE

ALPHABETS OF ANCIENT AND MODERN LANGUAGES

BASED ON THE GERMAN COMPILATION

OF

F. BALLHORN.

LONDON
TRÜBNER AND CO., 60, PATERNOSTER ROW.
1861.

PREFACE.

—◆—

THE GRAMMATOGRAPHY is offered to the Public as a compendious introduction to the reading of the most important ancient and modern languages. Simple in its design, it will be consulted with advantage by the Philological Student, the Amateur Linguist, the Bookseller, the Corrector of the Press, and the diligent Compositor.

Although substantially based on "Ballhorn's Alphabete," a German compilation, which, in the space of a few years, passed through nine editions, the present manual has in several articles been very considerably improved and enlarged. Of the new observations which have been inserted, some may prove useful even when this work shall be consulted by the side of the respective Grammars. With regard to the Asiatic Alphabets, it may be stated, that the continued efforts to obtain trustworthy specimens have, in some instances, led to highly satisfactory results. In preparing the type of the Chinese characters, the lateral "Tones" have been adjoined to the 214 symbols of pronunciation. These additions will enable the student, instructed by native teachers, to remember with greater facility the varying articulation of vowel-sounds.

The publishers entertain the hope, that the present work, an humble attempt to assist in the furtherance of philological pursuits, will obtain the encouraging consideration of competent scholars, whose suggestions, available for future editions, are respectfully solicited.

ALPHABETICAL INDEX.

PERSIAN CUNEIFORM CHARACTERS.

There are two main families of Cuneiform Characters which, before the expedition of Alexander the Great, were in use nearly in all Asiatic Countries, subjected to the (Achæmenides) Persian Kings. One of these, the Arian arrow-headed, is here given, and is a pure alphabet of fixed characters, which was made use of by the old Persians, proper, and is now read with tolerable accuracy. The other, however, not yet deciphered with sufficient certainty, was employed, with some modifications, by at least five different nations, the Babylonians, the Assyrians, the Medo-Scythians (the second in the triglot inscriptions of Persepolis and Bisutun), the Susians and the Armenians. Almost in each of these five sorts of characters can be distinguished three styles, the Archaic, the Lapidary, and the Cursive.

Form	Value	Form	Value	Form	Value	Form	Value
 𒀀	a	 𒀀	t	 𒀀	m before i	 𒀀	s (sh)
 𒀀	i	 𒀀	t' before i	 𒀀	m before u	 𒀀	z
 𒀀	u	 𒀀	t' before u	 𒀀	n	 𒀀	z', g'
 𒀀	k	 𒀀	th	 𒀀	y	 𒀀	h
 𒀀	q	 𒀀	d	 𒀀	r	 𒀀	thr (tr)
 𒀀	kh	 𒀀	dh	 𒀀	r'	 𒀀	rp, q
 𒀀	g	 𒀀	p	 �	f	 𒀀	d, h
 𒀀	gh	 �	f	 �	v	 �	b, u, m, i
 𒀀	k'	 �	b	 �	ç (s)	�	point for separating words.
 𒀀	g'	 �	m				

1

MEDIAN CUNEIFORM CHARACTERS

Form	Value	Form	Value	Form	Value	Form	Value
	a		t		phi		vo
	â		ta		y		s
	i		ti		yu		sa
	î		tu		yo		su
	u		th		r		s'
	û		thi		ra		s'a
	q		thu		ri		s'i
	qu		p		ru		z
	. k		pa		ro		za
	ka		pi		lu		h
	ku		pe		fi		ha
	kh		pu		fe		n
	kha		ph		v		ni
	khu		pha		vu		m

ASSYRIAN CUNEIFORM CHARACTERS

Form	Value	Form	Value	Form	Value	Form	Value
	a		ch		n		r
	a, ya		t		p		
	b		t, s				i rsh
	g, kh				ds, z, dsh or j		s
	d		i				
	h		i, y		k		
	hu, v, y		i, ü				sh
	u		y				
	o		kh				
	v, h, a, r		m, v		r		a, z
							nue
	ch		n				vush

OLDEST CHARACTERS

Arrangement	Hieroglyphics	Hieratic	Demotic	Phœnician	Numidian	Early - Hebrew
א Alĕph						
ב Bēth						
ג Gīmel						
ד Dāleth						
ה Hē						
ו Vāv						
ז Zāyĭn						
—						
—						
ח Chēth						
ט Tēth						
י Yōdh						
כ Kāph						
ל Lāmĕdh						
מ Mēm						
נ Nūn						
ס Sāmĕk						
ע Ayĭn						
פ Pō						
צ Tsādhē						
ק Q'ōph						
ר Rēsh						
ש Shīn						
ת Tāv						
ף						

OLDEST CHARACTERS

Aramaic	Estrangelo	Palmyrenian	Kufic	Old - Hellenic	Old - Italic	Etrurian	
ℵ ⅄	ܐ ܩ ܩ ܬ ܬ	ℵ ℵ ⅄	l	◁	◁ ⋔ ∧	ᴙ ᴀ	a
⅄		⅄	⌡	ᗺ ℬ	ᗺ ℬ	◇ ◖	
∧ ⅄		⅄	ζ	(Γ ⅂ ⅂	(⅂)	ᴀ ◲	
⅄		⅄	ᖯ	△ ▽ ▷	◁ ⅄ △	�8 ᗷ	b
⅄ ⅄		⅄	◢ ◢	⅀ E	⅀ ⅃ E	ᴋ ᴋ)	k, g
⅂ ⅂		⅂ ⅂	ᴤ	⅂ ⅄	⅃ ⅂ ⅂	⊃ᴋ⊂)	
⅃		I	⅃	I	⅄ ⅄	╬ ╠)	t, d
			ᴛ	H	⅄	⅄ ╠)	
				EI	...	⅀ ⅀	e
⊓		H	ᶘ	ᗷ H	ᗷ.H	ᗷ	f
◊	⅄	G	ᴗ	⊙	⊙ ⊖	ᗷ H	h
⋋ ⌃		⋋ ⊃	ᴖ	⅀ ⅀	⅄ ⅃	l i	i
⅄		ᴤ ᴧ	⅃	⋊ ᴋ	⋊ ᴋ	⅃⅃⅄)	l
⅃ ⅃		ᗷ	⅃	⅃ ⅃⅄	⅃ ⅃	⅃╫╫)	
ᴪ ᴪ		⅃	◦	⋔ ⋔	⋔	⋏ ᴄ)	m
⅄ ⅃		⅃	ᴧ	ᴧ	⅄ ᴧ	⋔ ⋔⋔)	
⅄		⅄ ⅄ ⅄	ᴝ	╬ I	╤	ᴎ ᴎ)	n
◡		⅄	ᴇ	◯	() ⊙	ᴦ ⅂)	
⅂		⅀ ⅃	ᴜ	⅂	⅂ ⅃	⅃ ⅃)	
⅄		⅄	ᴘ	⅀	⅄	⊖ ⊕)	o
						⊙ ◯)	
						⊘ ◇)	
P ⊤		ᴙ	ᴥ	ᴥ ᴥ	ᴥ ◦ △	⅃⅃⅃	p, b
⅄ ⅄		⅄ ⅄ ⅄	⅃	⅄ ⅄	◁ P	◁ ▽)	r
⅄		⅄	ᴝ	⋔ ⋔	⋔	ᴥᴅᴅ)	
ᖯ ᴛ		ᴘ	ᴊ	⅄ ⊤	╬ ╬	⅀⊃⅀	s
...			ᴁ	⅄ ⅄	⅄	⅄	u
						⅄ ⅄	v, u

HEBREW

Form	Name	Pronun-ciation	Numer.-value
א	Aleph	Spiritus lenis	1
ב	Beth	b bh	2
ג	Gimel	g gh	3
ד	Daleth	d dh	4
ה	He	h	5
ו	Vav	w	6
ז	Zayin	s soft	7
ח	Cheth	ch	8
ט	Teth	t	9
י	Yodh	j	10
כ, final ך	Kaph	k kh	20
ל	Lamedh	l	30
מ, final ם	Mem	m	40
נ, final ן	Nun	n	50
ס	Samek	s	60
ע	Ayin	guttural ·	70
פ, final ף	Pe	p ph	80
צ, final ץ	Tsadhe	ss	90
ק	Q'oph	q	100
ר	Resh	r	200
ש	Sin	s	300
ש	Shin	sh	
ת	Tav	t th	400

Final-Kaph
with Shva ךְ with Q'amets ךָ
with Daghesh and Q'amets ךּ

LIGATURES.
אֱ or אֳ = יְהֹוָה
אֱ = אֵל, also instead of אֱלֹהִים

NOTES.

The Hebrew Alphabet, like all Semitic alphabets, consists only of consonants, 22 in number, some of which, however, have also the force of vowels. Hebrew is read from right to left. Because at the end of the lines, words cannot be divided, the following dilatable characters (*dilatabiles*) were employed to help to justify, or fill up the lines; but now the practice is all but obsolete.

ם ה ל ה ה א

CONSONANTS.
Notes on Pronunciation.

א is the softest guttural, an emission of the breath scarcely to be heard, the Spiritus lenis of the Greeks, similar to ה, but much softer.

ה before a vowel, is our aspirated h (the Spiritus asper of the Greeks); but after a vowel, at the end of a syllable, it is a guttural, and, at the end of words, it often supplies the place of a vowel.

ע 1) is a guttural g, accompanied by a grating or rattling sound; 2) a softer breathing like א. In reading and transcribing hebrew words, it is now usual to omit ע and א, e. g. עֵלִי Eli.

ח is the harshest guttural, like the German ch as pronounced by the Swiss, or the Spanish x and j.

ר is pronounced in Hebrew more like a rattling guttural, than as a pure lingual, and partakes of both sounds.

ש and ש were originally but one and the same letter, as they still are when written without points; but as in some words this letter had a softer sound, similar to s, this two-fold pronunciation is distinguished by the grammarians by the diacritical point: שׁ (sh) and שׂ (s).

ז is the English z.

ט, ק and צ are strongly articulated sounds, produced by a compression of the lower organs of the mouth; the two first, therefore, differ essentially from ת and כ which are equivalent to our t and k, and are often aspirated.

The six consonants ב ג ד כ פ ת have a two-fold pronunciation: 1) a harder and more slender sound (tennis), like our b g d k p t, and 2) a smoother sound accompanied by a soft aspiration. The harder sound is the primeval; it occurs at the beginning of words and syllables without a vowel preceding immediately, and is indicated by a point (*Daghesh lene*) in those six consonants. They are aspirated after a vowel immediately preceding; in manuscripts this is indicated by the *Raphe* (‾), but in printed books the aspiration is shown by the absence of the Daghesh.

CLASSIFICATION OF THE CONSONANTS.

a) According to the organs of speech by which they are pronounced:
1) gutturals (*gutturales*) א ה ח ע ר
2) palatals (*palatinae*) י כ ג ק
3) linguals (*linguales*) ד ט ל נ ת and ז ס
4) dentals (*dentales*) ז ס צ ש
5) labials (*labiales*) ב ו מ פ
The ר partakes of the 1. and 3. classes.

b) According to their sound:
1) aspirated consonants (*aspirantes*): א ה ח ע
2) soft consonants (*molles*): liquids ל מ נ ר, semivowels ו י
3) sibilants (*sibilantes*): ז ס צ ש
4) mutes (*mutæ*): ב ג ד כ פ ת and ט ק

VOWELS.

That the scale of the five vowels â ê î o oo is derived from the three primitive vowels â î oo, is to be seen much more distinctly in the Hebrew and the other Semitic languages than in other languages. The ê has been formed by â + î, the o by â + oo, and, properly speaking, both are contracted diphthongs: ê = ai, ô = au. — The full vowels formed by this process are the following, arranged according to the three principal vowels and to their prosodical quantity:

Vowel ă (א)
ָ Q'amets, â ā
ַ Patach, à.

Vowel ê — î (י)
יֵ Tsere (with Yodh), ê
יִ Chireq (magnum), î
ֵ Tsere (without Yodh), ē (ě)
ֶ Seghol, ě, è (the latter is also written יֶ)
ִ Chireq (parvum), ĭ (i).

Vowel o — oo (ו)
וֹ Cholem (magnum), ô
וּ Shureq, û
ֹ Cholem (parvum), ō (ŏ)
ָ Q'amets-chatuph, ŭ
ֻ Q'ibbuts, ŏŏ (ŏŏ).

The vowels, or vowel-points, are placed under the consonants after which they are pronounced; but the Patach, placed under a guttural at the end of a word, is pronounced before this guttural, רוּחַ ruach, in which case it is named *Patach furtivum*. The Cholem (without Vav) is placed above the consonant on the left side: רֹ rō. The figure is to be pronounced sometimes *or*, the ז being consonant, and the ‾ preceding it: sometimes *oo*, the Cholem being read after the Vav. It is more accurate to distinguish thus: ז oo, ז oo, ז ô; likewise also ז (Shureq) and ז (Vav with Daghesh). (Shureq) is readily discernible, because a vowel neither can precede nor follow it, only this form is made use of.

In opposition to the vowels

ְ Shva (Sh°va) indicates the absence of a full and distinct vowel. Therefore

1) placed under a consonant concluding a syllable, it indicates the complete absence of a vowel and serves to divide the preceding syllable from the following (*Sh°va quiescens*). It is not made use of, however, when the consonant concluding the syllable at the same time concludes the word, except in the case of the Final Qoph (ך), and those words ending in two consonants, when each of them is to be furnished with a Sh°va, e. g. קָטַלְתְּ

2) it represents a slight and indistinct vowel, as it were only the onset or beginning of a vowel (*Sh°va mobile*).

The *Sh°va mobile* is pronounced somewhat more clear and distinct in the so called Chateph-vowels (חֲטֵף rapidum), joining a short vowel to the *Sh°va simplex*; in opposition to which it is also named *Sh°va compositum*. There are three Chatephs:

ֲ Chateph-Patach, half â
ֱ Chateph-Seghol, half ě
ֳ Chateph-Qamets, half o.

READING-SIGNS.

There are some reading-signs which have close connexion with the vowels and probably were introduced at the same time. Amongst these is to be noticed the diacritical point of שׁ and שׂ. Meeting together with the Cholem (ֹ), only one point is made use of which represents both; therefore שׂ is to be pronounced so, if no other vowel-point is added; and osh. when the preceding consonant is unpointed, e. g. שֹׂנֵא *sone*, מֹשֶׁה *mosheh*.

More frequently we see a point placed in the consonant to indicate in general a harder pronunciation. There are three cases to be distinguished, viz.:

Daghesh forte, doubling the consonants.

Daghesh lene, hardening the consonant; it stands only in the six *mutae*: נ כ פ ד ג ב in the above named cases; otherwise the point occurring in these consonants must be a *Daghesh forte*.

Mappiq, indicates that those consonants, which are also used as vowels, are then to be pronounced as consonants; in modern printing it is made use of only in the ה at the end of the words.

In opposition to the point hardening the consonant, a little stroke standing above the consonant indicates his softer sound. This stroke called

Raphe (ˉ) is now almost out of use, and is only employed in order to indicate expressly the absence of a *Daghesh* or *Mappiq*.

ACCENTS.

The general design of the accents is to indicate the rhythmical members of the verses in the Old Testament. In doing this, they perform a twofold duty; for the accents mark at one and the same time partly the logical relation of each word to the whole sentence, and partly the accented syllable of each single word. In the first case the accents supply the punctuation, in the latter they are signs of tone. — As *signs of tone*, the different accents are equivalent, because there is in Hebrew only one kind of accentuation. In most words, the last syllable is accented, more rarely the last but one. — As *signs of punctuation*, their use is more complicated, because they not only separate words, like our points, commas and colons, but also join one to the other. Therefore they are divided in *Distinctivi* and *Conjunctivi*. In the following list they are arranged not according to their grammatical value, but according to their being placed below the consonants or *above* them, in order to give a more facile view of them.

ACCENTS PLACED UNDER CONSONANTS.

˛ Silluq only at the end of the verse, therefore always joined with : Soph-pasuq, which stands between the single verses.

ˎ Athnach, mostly in the midst of a verse

˛ Yethibh (always to the left of the vowel).

˒ Tebhir

ˌ Tiphcha initiale

ˌ Merkha

ˌ Double-Merkha

˩ Munach

˛ Mahpakh (to the right of the vowel)

ˌ Darga

˅ Yärach

ˌ Tiphcha finale.

ACCENTS PLACED ABOVE CONSONANTS.

˒ Segholta

˒ Zaqeph-qaton

˵ Zaqeph-gadhol

˙ Rebhia

˜ Zarqa

˒ Qadma

˒ Pashta

˛ Shalshelet

ˇ Paser

˅ Qarne-phara

˒ Great-Telisha

˥ Little-Telisha

˒ Gāresh

˝ Double-Gāresh.

ACCENTS CONSISTING OF TWO PARTS BELONGING TOGETHER, THE ONE ABOVE, AND THE OTHER BELOW CONSONANTS.

Merkha mahpakhatum

Merkha sarqatum

Mahpakh sarqatum.

: Soph-pasuq, separating verses.

׀ Pesiq, between the words.

- Maqqeph, hyphen, aloft, between the words.

ˌ Methog, sign of tone (to the left of the vowel).

NUMERALS.

There are no numerical ciphers in Hebrew; but consonants are used instead of them. The units are expressed by א — ט, the tens by י — צ, 100 — 400 by ק — ת. The numbers 500—900 sometimes are expressed by the five final letters ך 500, ם 600, ן 700, ף 800, ץ 900, sometimes by ת = 400 with addition of the other hundreds, e. g. תק = 500. In compound numbers, the greater is placed first, e. g. יא 11, קכא 121. The number 15 is written with טו (9 + 6), instead of יה, because the name of God יהוה begins with these letters; and for the same reason, 16 is written טז instead of יו. The thousands are expressed by the units, superscribing two points, e. g. אׄ 1000.

ABBREVIATIONS.

′ A stroke aloft to the left of the consonant, e. g. א′, denotes that this consonant serves as a numeral. By the side of the last consonant of a word, e. g. מס′ (= מסורה) it marks an abbreviation.

″ Two strokes above a word, e. g. א″ה, indicate that each of these letters stands for a separate word abbreviated.

ᵒ or ＊ in copies of the Hebrew Bible refer to the readings placed in the margin or at the foot of the page. The first is of Masoretic, and the other is of modern origin.

RABBINIC

Form	Name	Pronunciation
ﬡ	Aleph	Spiritus lenis
ﬄ	Beth	bh b
ﬠ	Gimel	gh g
ﬢ	Daleth	dh d
ﬣ	He	h
ﬢ	Vav	w
ﬤ	Zayin	s
ﬡ	Cheth	ch guttural
ﬢ	Teth	t
ﬧ	Yodh	y
ﬡ, final ﬡ	Kaph	ch k
ﬡ	Lamedh	l
ﬡ, final ﬡ	Mem	m
ﬡ, final ﬡ	Nun	n
ﬡ	Samek	s
ﬢ	Ayin	guttural
ﬡ, final ﬡ	Pe	ph p
ﬡ, final ﬡ	Tsadhe	z
ﬧ	Q'oph	k
ﬧ	Resh	r
ﬡ	Shin Sin	sh s
ﬡ	Tav	th t

GERMAN-RABBINIC

Form	Pronunciation
ﬡ	a
ﬤ	b
ﬥ	v f
ﬦ	g
ﬧ	d
ﬨ	h
﬩	v u o
ﬡ	w
ﬢ	s
ﬡ	cch
ﬢ	t
ﬧ	i j e short
ﬡ, final ﬡ	c
ﬢ	ch
ﬣ	l
ﬡ, final ﬡ	m
ﬡ, final ﬡ	n
ﬡ	s ss
ﬢ	c long
ﬡ, final ﬡ	p
ﬤ	ph pf v
ﬡ, final ﬡ	z tz
ﬧ	k ck q
ﬧ	r
ﬡ	s sh
ﬢ	t
ﬣ	tt

DIPHTHONGS.

ﬡﬢ au, ﬢ ei, ﬢﬢ eu, ﬢ ö ü german.

HEBREW RUNNING-HAND

Form		Name	Pronun-ciation		Numerical value	Ligatures			
Polish	German								
ϰ	ʎ	Aleph	א	a	1				
ʰ	₴	Beth	ב	b	2	℗	=	בע	be
∕	∕	Gimel	ג	g	3	𝓧	=	בה	bh
૧	૧	Daleth	ד	d	4				
૧	૨	He	ה	h	5	℘	=	גג	ng
׀	׀	Vav	ו	w	6	ℊ	=	גד	nd
׃	₂	Zayin .	ז	s	7				
ח	ח	Cheth	ח	ch	8	ℴ	=	גה	nh
ƅ	ƅ	Teth	ט	t	9	℗	=	גפ	nf
ʾ	ʾ	Yodh	י	y	10	ℳ	=	גג	nn
Ɔ	Ɔ	Kaph	כ	cch	20				
∫	∫ or ₵	Lamedh	ל	l	30	ℴ	=	גו	nw
∎	∎	Mem	מ	m	40	ℐ	=	גי	nj
⌐	⌐	Nun	נ	n	50				
ο	ο	Samek	ס	ss	60	ℰ	=	צד	zd
∮ or ϰ	∮ or ϰ	Ayin	ע	c	70	℥	=	צו	zw
ϑ	Ϭ	Pe	פ	p	80	ℨ	=	צי	zi
ϑ̃	ϑ̃	Fe	פֿ	f	90				
ℨ	ℨ	Tsadhe	צ	c or z	100	℘ l with mark of abbreviation, in use at the end of certain words.			
ℓ	ℓ	Q'oph	ק	k	200				
⌐	⌐	Resh	ר	r	300				
Ϙ	Ϙ	Shin	ש	sh	400				
⅃	⅃	Tav	ת	th	500				

FINAL LETTERS.

Polish.				German.			
ℙ	=	ך	cch	ℙ	=	ך	cch
℘	=	ם	m	℘	=	ם	m
(	=	ן	n	(	=	ן	n
ℬ	=	ף	f	℘ ℰ ℨ	=	ף	f
℘	=	ץ	c z	ℙ ℙ	=	ץ	c z

SAMARITAN

Form	Name	Pronun-ciation	Numerical value
ℵ	Aleph	Spiritus lenis	1
𝟗	Beth	b bh	2
𝟀	Gimel	g gh	3
𝟓	Daleth	d dh	4
𝟑	He	h Spir. asper	5
𝟀	Vav	w v	6
𝔰	Zayin	s ds	7
𝔥	Cheth	ch hh	8
▽	Teth	t	9
𝔪	Yodh	y	10
𝔲	Kaph	k ch	20
𝟐	Lamedh	l	30
𝔴	Mem	m	40
𝟏	Nun	n	50
𝔰	Samek	s	60
▽	Ayin	ע hebrew	70
𝔍	Pe	p ph	80
𝔪	Tsadhe	ts	90
𝟈	Q'oph	k	100
𝟗	Resh	r	200
ɯ	Shin	sh	300
ℵ	Tav	t th	400

NOTES.

The Samaritan is a Semitic language. Therefore, the alphabet consists only of consonants (22 in number) and is read from right to left. As in this language words cannot be separated at the end of the lines, the two letters ending the last word are separated from the others and placed at the end of the line; but in printing this is generally avoided by diminishing or enlarging the spaces between the single words.

Save some points and scanty orthographical signs, there are in Samaritan no vowel-marks, accents or other diacritical signs as in Hebrew. Therefore we are somewhat in the dark about the pronunciation of the consonants and vowels and it can be acquired only by comparison with the Syriac and the Hebrew.

VOWELS.

There are no vowel-marks as in other Semitic languages. However, to supply this want and to indicate somewhat the pronunciation, some consonants are used as vowels, viz.:

$$\text{a } ℵ, 𝟑, ▽$$
$$\text{ə } ℵ, 𝔪$$
$$\text{ɪ } 𝔪$$
$$\text{o, oo } 𝟀$$

Of two consonants beginning a word, the first is pronounced as if it were a slight and indistinct vowel, similar to the Hebrew Shwa.

DIACRITICAL SIGNS.

The only diacritical sign is a stroke over the consonant (e. g. ℵ̄) serving to distinguish two different words written in the same manner, or two different forms derived from one and the same root, or to indicate some letter added or omitted. When placed over 𝔪 or 𝟀, the stroke indicates that these letters are real consonants, not representing vowels.

PUNCTUATION.

A point is put by the side of the final letter of a word. Besides this, the following signs have been introduced by the transcribers:

: or ˙ or ·: at the end of a sentence,

·· (also ·) at the end of part of a sentence, like our colon,

=·: or —<: more seldom —·: etc., or compound —<: =·: etc at the end of a longer sentence or section,

<·:==·:> or similar signs, sometimes again and again repeated, between the end of one section, paragraph or chapter, and the beginning of the other,

The numbers are written as in Hebrew (see under).

SYRIAC

Name	Form uncon-nected	Form connect-ed with a preced-ing letter	Form connect-ed with both	Form connect-ed with a follow-ing letter	Pronun-ciation	Numer. value
Olaph	ı	ᴸ	. . .	. . .	Spiritus lenis	1
Beth	︔	︔	︔	︔	b or v	2
Gomal	⟍	⟍	⟍	⟍	g	3
Dolath	?	ᴿ	. . .	. . .	d	4
He	ᑕ	ᑕ	. . .	. . .	h	5
Vau	o	ꭥ	. . .	. . .	w or v	6
Zain	ı	ⵏ	. . .	. . .	z	7
Cheth	◢◣	◢◣	◢◣	◢◣	ch	8
Teth	◢	◢	◢	◢	t	9
Yud	◣	◣	◣	◣	y	10
Koph	ⲩ	ⲩ	◔	◔	ch	20
Lomad	⟍	⟍	⟍	⟍	l	30
Mim	⅋	⅋	⅋	⅋	m	40
Nun	⟍	⟍	ⵏ	ⵏ	n	50
Semcath	◫	◫	◫	◫	s	60
Ee	⟍	⟍	⟍	⟍	y as in hebrew	70
Pe	︔	︔	◔	◔	p or f	80
Tsodé	⟋	⟋	. . .	. . .	ts or z	90
Quph	◔	◔	◔	◔	q	100
Rish	;	;	. . .	. . .	r	200
Shin	◢◣	◢◣	◢◣	◢◣	sh	300
Tau	⟋	ᐃ	. . .	. . .	th or t	400

VOWELS.

The Syriac is written from right to left. — The vowels are expressed by diacritical signs or some marks in imitation of the greek; the latter of which are now mostly in use. In former times both kinds were employed promiscuously.

Figure Syriac.	Figure Greek.	Name	Pronun-ciation.
⫶	𝑉	Pethocho	ă
⁚ or ⁚	⁀	Rebotzo	ĕ
⫶	⁀	Chebotzo	ī
⁾ or ⁾	⸜	Zekopho	o
ḍ ḍ ḍ	ꭥ ⟍	Etsotso	oo

DIACRITICAL SIGNS.

. *Ruchoch*, a point below an aspirated letter to indicate that it is to be aspirated.
· *Quakof*, a little point over an aspirated letter to indicate that it is not to be aspirated.
·· *Ribui*, two points placed horizontally above the word to indicate the plural.
— *Marhetono*, a line above a letter between two consonants to indicate the absence of a vowel. Besides, this line signifies 1) a number, 2) an abbreviation, 3) an exclamation.
— *Mehagyono*, a line below a letter, to show that though without a vowel it is to be pronounced as if it had one.
— *Linea occultans*, a line placed below a letter to denote that it is to be mute or omitted in pronunciation.

PUNCTUATION.

⁚ marks a single part of the premise of a sentence.
⸴ marks the end of a premise; or, it is sign of interrogation.
⸴' marks the single parts of the conclusion of a sentence; or, larger interrogations.
❖ or ⁚⁚ at the end of a period.

NUMERICAL VALUE.

The consonants of the alphabet supply the numbers from 1 to 400; in compound numbers, the greater precedes. Within 500 — 900, the tens from 50 — 90 are denoted by a point standing aloft. The mark ⸜ under a unit denotes the thousands, ⸴ the ten-thousands, ⤳ the product of the thousands multiplied by the tenthousands. In writing fractions, the numerator is denoted by a little stroke going from left to right, placed above the denominator.

LIGATURES.

⟍ ⟍ Olaph-Lomad.   ꭥ ✕ ꭥ ✕ Lomad-Olaph.   ⟍ Double-Gomal.   ⟍⟍ Double-Lomad.

SYRIAC

Cut in the printing-office of B. G. TEUBNER in Leipzig conformably to original drawings by Professor TULLBERG of Upsala and Professor BRUNSTEIN of Breslau.

Form	Pronun-ciation	Name	Form	Pronun-ciation	Name	Form	Pronun-ciation	Name
1			29			57		
2	a or Spirit. lenis.	Olaph	30	gh	Gomal	58	z (gr. ζ)	Zain
3			31			59		
4			32			60		
5			33			61	kh	Cheth
6	b and bh		34	d and dh		62		
7			35			63		
8			36			64		
9			37			65		
10			38			66		
11		Beth	39	d	Dolath	67	t	Teth
12	b		40			68		
13			41			69		
14			42	or		70		
15			43	or		71		
16	bh		44	dh		72		
17			45			73		
18			46			74	i	Yud
19			47			75		
20	g and gh		48			76		
21			49			77		
22			50	h	He	78		
23			51			79		
24		Gomal	52			80	c and ch	Koph
25	g		53			81		
26			54			82		
27			55	w v u	Vau	83		
28	gh		56			84	c	

SYRIAC

Form	Pronunciation	Name	Form	Pronunciation	Name	Form	Pronunciation	Name
85			115			145		
86			116	s	Semeath	146	sh	Shin
87	c		117			147		
88			118			148		
89			119			149	t and th	
90		Koph	120	ee (hebr. ע)	Ee	150		
91			121			151		
92	ch		122			152		
93			123			153		
94			124			154	t	Tau
95			125	p and ph(f)		155		
96			126			156		
97			127		Phe	157		
98	l	Lomad	128			158	th	
99			129	p		159		
100			130			160		
101			131	ph f				
102			132			**LIGATURES.**		
103			133	Sharp s or ss	Tsodé	161	al	Olaph-Lomad
104			134			162		
105	m	Mim	135			163		
106			136			164		
107	,		137	k	Quph	165		
108			138			166	gg	Double-Gomul
109			139			167		
110	n	Nun	140			168		
111			141	r	Rish	169		
112			142			170	gv	Gomal-Vau
113			143			171		
114	s	Semcath	144	sh	Shin	172	vn	Vau-Nun
						173		

SYRIAC

Form	Pronunciation	Name	Vowels, Accents and Orthographical Signs		Points and Numbers	
174 ⲥ	in	Yud-Nun	**VOWELS AND ACCENTS.**		**POINTS.**	
175 ⲥ			203		224 .	229 .·
176 ⲗ			204	a Pethocho	225 _:	230 ⋮
177 ⲗ	la	Lomad-Olaph	205		226 ⁻:	231 ·.
178 ⲭ			206	e Rebotzo	227 _·.	232 ⋄
179 ⲭ			207		228 ⁻·.	
180 ⲁ			208		233 ⸯ Mark of marginal	
181 ⲁ	lt	Lomad-Teth	209	i Chebotzo	notes	
182 ⲁ			210		234 ⸯ Number-Mark	
183 ⲁ			211			
184 ⲗ			212	o Zekopho	**NUMBERS.**	
185 ⲗ			213		Form	Value
186 ⲗ	ll	Double Lomad	214	u Etsotso	ⲓ	1
187 ⲗ					ⲟ	2
188 ⲗ					ⲩ	3
189 ⲗ			**ORTHOGRAPHICAL SIGNS.**		ⲥ	4
190 ⲗ	lee	Lomad-Ee			ⲟ	5
191 ⲗ			215 .. Ribui		ⲟ	6
192 ⲗ			216 - Mehagyono		ⲓ	7
193 ⲗ			217 — Marhetono		ⲩ	8
194 ⲗ	lt	Lomad-Tau	218 Qushoi, Ruchoch		ⲫ	9
195 ⲗ					ⲩ	10
196 ⲗ					ⲫ	20
197 ⲩ	mn	Mim-Nun	219 . Little hooks at the beginning of a word		ⲗ	30
198 ⲗ	na	Nun-Olaph	220 . at the end of a word		ⲗ	40
199 ⲗ			221 ,		ⲩ	50
200 ⲭ	ssn	Tsodé-Nun	222 . Strokes between the single letters to adjust the lines		ⲫ	60
			223 —		ⲩ	70
201 ⲭ	ssg	Tsodé-Gomal			ⲫ	80
202 ⲭ					ⲗ	90
					ⲫ	100
					ⲓ	200
					ⲗ	300
					ⲗ	400
					ⲓ	1000

3 *

ARABIC

Name	Form				Pronunciation	Numerical value
	Unconnected	Connected with a preceding letter	Connected with both	Connected with a following letter		
Elif	ا	ل			א Spir. lenis	1
Ba	ب	ب	٠	ب	b	2
Ta	ت	ت	ت	ث	t	400
Tha	ث	ث	ث	ث	th	500
Jim	ج	ج	ج	ج	j	3
Hha	ح	ح	ح	ح	hh	8
Cha	خ	خ	خ	خ	ch	600
Dal	د	د			d	4
Dhal	ذ	ذ			dh or ds	700
Ra	ر	ر ‍ر			r	200
Zay	ز	ز			z	7
Sin	س	س	س	س	s	60
Shin	ش	ش	ش	ش	sh	300
Ssad	ص	ص	ص	ص	ss or ç	90
Ddad	ض	ض	ض	ض	d or dd	800
Tta	ط	ط	ط	ط	tt or th	9
Zza	ظ	ظ	ظ	ظ	zz	900
Ain	ع	ع	ع	ع	ע Spir. gutt.	70
Ghain	غ	غ	غ	غ	gh	1000
Fa	ف	ف	ف	ف	f	80
Qaf	ق	ق	ق	ق	k	100
Kaf	ك	ك	ك ‍ك	ك ‍ك	k soft	20
Lam	ل	ل	ل	ل	l	30
Mim	م	م	م	م	m	40
Nun	ن	ن	ن	ن	n	50
Ha	ة Final ة	ة Final ة	ه	ه	h	5
Waw	و	و	. . .		w	6
Ya	ي	ي	ي	ي	y, i	10

ORTHOGRAPHICAL SIGNS

VOWELS.

⌣ Fatha, ä ä ĕ ⌣ Kesre, ĭ ĕ ⌣ Damma, oo o

At the end of the substantives the vowels are doubled to indicate the case, viz.:

⌣ on ⌣ in ⌣ an

This is called *Nunation*, because, in pronouncing, Nun is added to the vowel.

DIPHTHONGS: ◌ ai ◌ au as in german.

ORTHOGRAPHICAL SIGNS.

⌣ **Jezma**, separating syllables, is written over the final consonant of all shut syllable and indicates, that the syllable is finished and the consonant to be pronounced with the preceding vowel; it corresponds to the *Shwa quiescens* of the Hebrew.

⌣ **Teshdid**, mark of doubling. The final consonant of a syllable being the same as that beginning the following one, this consonant is written only once, but marked with the sign ⌣, which corresponds to the Hebrew *Daghesh forte*. In African manuscripts it is written v or ʌ.

⌣ **Hamza** is placed generally above the Elif, when this is used as a consonant and furnished with a vowel; when this vowel is a Kesre, the Hamza is placed beneath; sometimes also it stands above the Y. In Kufic Korans it is supplied by a little green stroke, in Moorish or African manuscripts by a thick green or yellow dot.

⌣ **Wesla**, joining-mark. The Elif, at the commencement of a word, is sometimes in pronunciation absorbed by the final vowel of the preceding word. In this case, the vowel of the Elif is elided and marked by the Wesla.

⌣ **Medda** stands above an Elif pronounced by Fatha and followed by a Hamza; it indicates the prolongation of the a. It is placed, also, above an Elif at the commencement of a word, or instead of an omitted Elif. Besides, this sign is a mark of abbreviation.

PUNCTUATION.

There are no signs of punctuation in Arabic, only in the Koran the verses are separated by ✿. This sign, however, or ʿ or ⸲ or a red dot, is employed also in other books at the end of a section. In manuscripts, sometimes, a new section begins with a word written in red colour; in manuscript dictionaries a red line is placed above each catch-word.

CIPHERS.

Formerly, the Arabs, like other oriental nations, used the letters of the alphabet to express numbers; at a later period, however, they adopted the following 10 special figures, called by us Europeans the Arabian ciphers, by the Arabs themselves the Indian ones.

١	٢	٣	٤	٥	٦	٧	٨	٩	٠
1	2	3	4	5	6	7	8	9	0

Regarding their composition and value they accord with our numerals, which are taken from them, whereas the consonants expressing ciphers are written from right to left, viz. ١٨٦١ (1861).

ARABIC LIGATURES

Ba-Jim		Tha-Cha
Ba-Hha		Jim-Jim
Ba-Hha-Jim		Jim-Hha
Ba-Cha		Hha-Jim
Ta-Jim		Hha-Jim-Jim
Ta-Hha		Hha-Jim-Hha
Ta-Cha		Hha-Hha
Tha-Hha		Hha-Hha-Jim

ARABIC LIGATURES

		چ	حـ	Hha-Cha			كـ	كـ	Kaf-Cha
		چ	جـ	Cha-Jim			لا	لا	Lam-Elif
		چ	حـ	Cha-Hha		چ	جـ	لـ	Lam-Jim
چ	جـ	سـ	سـ	Sin-Jim				لـ	Lam-Jim-Hha
چ	چ	سـ	سـ	Sin-Hha		چ	حـ	لـ	Lam-Hha
چ	چ	سـ	سـ	Sin-Cha				لـ	Lam-Hha-Jim
چ	چ	شـ	شـ	Shin-Jim				لـ	Lam-Hha-Hha
چ	چ	شـ	شـ	Shin-Hha		چ	حـ	لـ	Lam-Cha
		چ	شـ	Shin-Cha				لـ	Lam-Cha-Jim
چ	چ	صـ	صـ	Ssad-Jim				لم	Lam-Mim-Hha-Jim
چ	چ	صـ	صـ	Ssad-Hha				لم	Lam-Mim-Hha-Hha
چ	چ	صـ	صـ	Ssad-Cha			لى	لى	Lam-Ya
			ضـ	Ddad-Jim		چ	مـ	مـ	Mim-Jim
		ضـ	ضـ	Ddad-Hha		چ	مـ	مـ	Mim-Hha
		طـ	طـ	Tta-Hha				مـ	Mim-Hha-Jim
		عـ	عـ	Ain-Jim				مـ	Mim-Hha-Hha
		عـ	عـ	Ain-Hha		چ	مـ	مـ	Mim-Cha
		غـ	غـ	Ghain-Jim		چ	نـ	نـ	Nun-Jim
		غـ	غـ	Ghain-Hha		چ	نـ	نـ	Nun-Hha
چ	چ	فـ	فـ	Fa-Jim			نـ	نـ	Nun-Cha
چ	چ	فـ	فـ	Fa-Hha			هـ	هـ	Ha-Jim
چ	چ	فـ	فـ	Fa-Cha			هـ	هـ	Ha-Hha
			فى	Fa-Ya			هـ	هـ	Ha-Cha
		قـ	قـ	Qaf-Jim				هم	Ha-Mim
		قـ	قـ	Qaf-Hha		چ	يـ	يـ	Ya-Jim
		قـ	قـ	Qaf-Cha				يـ	Ya-Jim-Hha
		كا	كا	Kaf-Elif		چ	يـ	يـ	Ya-Hha
		كـ	كـ	Kaf-Jim				يـ	Ya-Hha-Hha
		كـ	كـ	Kaf-Hha			يـ	يـ	Ya-Cha

AETHIOPIAN AND AMHARIC

Name	Form							Pronun-ciation
	with ā	with ū	with ī	with â	with ê	with ĕ	with ô	
Hoi	U ha	U· hu	ሂ hi	ሃ hā	ሄ he	U he	ሆ ho	h
Lawi	ለ la	ሉ lu	ሊ li	ላ la	ሌ le	ለ le	ሎ lo	l
Haut	ሐ ha	ሑ hu	ሒ hi	ሓ ha	ሔ he	ሕ he	ሖ ho	h
Mai	መ ma	ሙ mu	ሚ mi	ማ ma	ሜ me	ም me	ሞ mo	m
Saut	ሠ sā	ሡ su	ሢ si	ሣ sa	ሤ se	ሥ se	ሦ so	s
Rees	ረ ra	ሩ ru	ሪ ri	ራ ra	ሬ re	ር re	ሮ ro	r
Sat	ሰ sa	ሱ su	ሲ si	ሳ sa	ሴ se	ስ se	ሶ so	s
*Shat	ሸ sha	ሹ sha	ሺ shi	ሻ sha	ሼ she	ሽ she	ሾ sho	sh
Kaf	ቀ ka	ቁ ku	ቂ ki	ቃ ka	ቄ ke	ቅ ke	ቆ ko	k
Bet	በ ba	ቡ bu	ቢ bi	ባ ba	ቤ be	ብ be	ቦ bo	b
Tawi	ተ ta	ቱ tu	ቲ ti	ታ ta	ቴ te	ት te	ቶ to	t
*Tshawi	ቸ tsha	ቹ tshu	ቺ tshi	ቻ tsha	ቼ tshe	ች tshe	ቾ tsho	tsh
Harm	ኀ ha	ኁ hu	ኂ hi	ኃ ha	ኄ he	ኅ he	ኆ ho	h
Nahas	ነ na	ኑ nu	ኒ ni	ና na	ኔ ne	ን ne	ኖ no	n
*Gnahas	ኘ gna	ኙ gnu	ኚ gni	ኛ gna	ኜ gne	ኝ gne	ኞ gno	gn
Alf	አ a	ኡ u	ኢ i	ኣ a	ኤ e	እ e	ኦ o	a
Kaf	ከ ka	ኩ ku	ኪ ki	ካ ka	ኬ ke	ክ ke	ኮ ko	k
*Chaf	ኸ cha	ኹ chu	ኺ chi	ኻ cha	ኼ che	ኽ che	ኾ cho	ch
Wawi	ወ wa	ዉ wu	ዊ wi	ዋ wa	ዌ we	ው we	ዎ wo	w
Ain	ዐ a	ዑ u	ዒ i	ዓ a	ዔ e	ዕ e	ዖ o	y
Zai	ዘ za	ዙ zu	ዚ zi	ዛ za	ዜ ze	ዝ ze	ዞ zo	z
*Zshai	ዠ ja	ዡ ju	ዢ ji	ዣ ja	ዤ je	ዥ je	ዦ jo	j fr.
Yaman	የ ya	ዩ yu	ዪ yi	ያ ya	ዬ ye	ይ ye	ዮ yo	y
Dent	ደ da	ዱ du	ዲ di	ዳ da	ዴ de	ድ de	ዶ do	d
*Jent	ጀ ja	ጁ ju	ጂ ji	ጃ ja	ጄ je	ጅ je	ጆ jo	j
Geml	ገ ga	ጉ gu	ጊ gi	ጋ ga	ጌ ge	ግ ge	ጎ go	g
Tait	ጠ ta	ጡ tu	ጢ ti	ጣ ta	ጤ te	ጥ te	ጦ to	t
*Tshait	ጨ tsha	ጩ tshu	ጪ tshi	ጫ tsha	ጬ tshe	ጭ tshe	ጮ tsho	tsh
Pait	ጰ pa	ጱ pu	ጲ pi	ጳ pa	ጴ pe	ጵ pe	ጶ po	p
Tzadai	ጸ tsa	ጹ tsu	ጺ tsi	ጻ tsa	ጼ tse	ጽ tse	ጾ tso	ts
Tsappa	ፀ tsa	ፁ tsu	ፂ tsi	ፃ tsa	ፄ tse	ፅ tse	ፆ tso	ts
Aff	ፈ fa	ፉ fu	ፊ fi	ፋ fa	ፌ fe	ፍ fe	ፎ fo	f
Pa	ፐ pa	ፑ pu	ፒ pi	ፓ pa	ፔ pe	ፕ pe	ፖ po	p

DIPHTHONGS.

ቈ	kua	ቊ	kui	ቋ	kua	ቌ	kue	ቍ	kue
ኈ	hhua	ኊ	hhui	ኋ	hhua	ኌ	hhue	ኍ	hhue
ኰ	kua	ኲ	kui	ኳ	kua	ኴ	kue	ኵ	kue
ጐ	gua	ጒ	gui	ጓ	gua	ጔ	gue	ጕ	gue

NOTE.
The Aethiopian and the Amharic are read from left to right. The words are separated by:—The alphabet of both languages is syllabic; the Amharic, however, has seven orders of letters (each order consisting of 7 forms or characters), wanting in Aethiopian, which, in the above table, are marked by *.

AETHIOPIAN

Cut in the printing-office of F. A. Brockhaus in Leipzig under the direction of the German Oriental Society.

With ā		With û		With î		With ă		With ė		With ĕ		With ô	
ሀ	ha	ሁ	hù	ሂ	hî	ሃ	hà	ሄ	hė	ህ	he	ሆ	hò
ለ	la	ሉ	lù	ሊ	li	ላ	là	ሌ	lė	ል	le	ሎ	lò
ሐ	ha	ሑ	hù	ሒ	hî	ሓ	hà	ሔ	hė	ሕ	he	ሖ	hò
መ	ma	ሙ	mù	ሚ	mî	ማ	mà	ሜ	mė	ም	me	ሞ	mò
ሠ	śa	ሡ	śù	ሢ	śî	ሣ	śà	ሤ	śė	ሥ	śe	ሦ	śò
ረ	ra	ሩ	rù	ሪ	rî	ራ	rà	ሬ	rė	ር	re	ሮ	rò
ሰ	sa	ሱ	sù	ሲ	sî	ሳ	sà	ሴ	sė	ስ	se	ሶ	sò
ቀ	qa	ቁ	qù	ቂ	qî	ቃ	qà	ቄ	qė	ቅ	qe	ቆ	qò
በ	ba	ቡ	bù	ቢ	bî	ባ	bà	ቤ	bė	ብ	be	ቦ	bò
ተ	ta	ቱ	tù	ቲ	tî	ታ	tà	ቴ	tė	ት	te	ቶ	tò
ኀ	ha	ኁ	hù	ኂ	hî	ኃ	hà	ኄ	hė	ኅ	he	ኆ	hò
ነ	na	ኑ	nù	ኒ	nî	ና	nà	ኔ	nė	ን	ne	ኖ	nò
አ	-a	ኡ	-ù	ኢ	-î	ኣ	-à	ኤ	-ė	እ	-e	ኦ	-ò
ከ	ka	ኩ	kù	ኪ	kî	ካ	kà	ኬ	kė	ክ	ke	ኮ	kò
ወ	wa	ዉ	wù	ዊ	wî	ዋ	wà	ዌ	wė	ው	we	ዎ	wò
ዐ	a	ዑ	ʿù	ዒ	ʿî	ዓ	ʿà	ዔ	ʿė	ዕ	ʿe	ዖ	ʿò
ዘ	za	ዙ	zù	ዚ	zî	ዛ	zà	ዜ	zė	ዝ	ze,	ዞ	zò
የ	ya	ዩ	yù	ዪ	yî	ያ	yà	ዬ	yė	ይ	ye	ዮ	yò
ደ	da	ዱ	dù	ዲ	dî	ዳ	dà	ዴ	dė	ድ	de	ዶ	dò
ገ	ga	ጉ	gù	ጊ	gî	ጋ	gà	ጌ	gė	ግ	ge	ጎ	gò
ጠ	ṭa	ጡ	ṭù	ጢ	ṭî	ጣ	ṭà	ጤ	ṭė	ጥ	ṭe	ጦ	ṭò
ጰ	ṗa	ጱ	ṗù	ጲ	ṗî	ጳ	ṗà	ጴ	ṗė	ጵ	ṗe	ጶ	ṗò
ጸ	za	ጹ	zù	ጺ	zî	ጻ	zà	ጼ	zė	ጽ	ze	ጾ	zò
ፀ	za	ፁ	zù	ፂ	zî	ፃ	zà	ፄ	zė	ፅ	ze	ፆ	zò
ፈ	fa	ፉ	fù	ፊ	fî	ፋ	fà	ፌ	fė	ፍ	fe	ፎ	fò
ፐ	pa	ፑ	pù	ፒ	pî	ፓ	pà	ፔ	pė	ፕ	pe	ፖ	pò

DIPHTHONGS.

ⷈ	kua	ⷉ	kui	ⷊ	kue	ⷋ	kuà	ⷌ	kué
ⷉ	gua	ⷈ	gui	ⷊ	gue	ⷋ	guà	ⷌ	gué
ⷄ	qua	ⷅ	qui	ⷆ	que	⷇	quà	ⷈ	qué
ⷎ	hua	⷏	hui	ⷐ	hue	ⷑ	huà	ⷒ	hué

PUNCTUATION.

፡ Stop for the division of words ፤ Comma ፥ Semicolon ። Full stop

NUMBERS.

፩	፪	፫	፬	፭	፮	፯	፰	፱	፲	፲፩ etc.	፳	፴	፵	፶	፷	፸	፹	፺	፻	፻፪ etc.	፲፻	፲፻፻	፻፻	፲፻፻፻
1	2	3	4	5	6	7	8	9	10	11 etc.	20	30	40	50	60	70	80	90	100	200 etc.	1000	10,000	100,000	1,000.000

Ethiopic, formerly the vernacular language of the Abyssinians, by whom it was called Gëez, is only preserved in writings. As a Semitic language it bears a close affinity to the Himyaric, a South-Arabian dialect, which was superseded in the times of Mahomed. The Ethiopic possesses a high degree of flexibility which is mainly due to the diligence with which the study of Greek writings was cultivated in Abyssinia. The Alphabet originally consisted of consonants without indications of vowels. In form it approaches the Himyaric and thus differs from the other Semitic characters. Ancient Ethiopic inscriptions show examples of writing from right to left; owing, however, to the early influence of Greek literature, especially after the introduction of Christianity, the arrangement of words was fixed from left to right. At the same time the coalition of consonants and vowels was indicated by particular forms, which gave rise to the adoption of a complete syllabarium. With the change of the ruling power in the fourteenth century the Ethiopic language began to decay, and rapidly falling into disuse, it is now replaced by the Amharic language.

AMHARIC.

This language deriving its name from the kingdom of Amhara in Abyssinia, has supplanted the ancient Ethiopic idiom. The kings of Shoa, on gaining the upper hand, effected the preponderance of the Amharic language, to the exclusion of the kindred Ethiopic. The Alphabets of both languages are identical, except the following Characters, which are peculiar to the Amharic language.

with a		with û		with î		with û		with ê		with e		with ô	
ሸ	sha	ሹ	shù	ሺ	shi	ሻ	shà	ሼ	shé	ሽ	she	ሾ	shô
ቸ	tsha	ቹ	tshù	ቺ	tshi	ቻ	tshà	ቼ	tshé	ች	tshe	ቾ	tshô
ኘ	ña	ኙ	ñù	ኚ	ñi	ኛ	ñà	ኜ	ñé	ኝ	ñe	ኞ	ñô
ኸ	kha	ኹ	khù	ኺ	khi	ኻ	khà	ኼ	khé	ኽ	khe	ኾ	khô
ዠ	ja (Fr.)	ዡ	jù	ዢ	ji	ዣ	jà	ዤ	jé	ዥ	je	ዦ	jò
ጀ	ja	ጁ	jù	ጂ	ji	ጃ	jà	ጄ	jé	ጅ	je	ጆ	jô
ጨ	chha	ጩ	chhù	ጪ	chhi	ጫ	chhà	ጬ	chhé	ጭ	chhe	ጮ	chhô

DIPHTHONGS.

ሏ	lua	ሿ	šua	ኋ	nua	ጧ	tua
ሟ	mua	ቧ	bua	ዟ	zua	ቯ	çua
ሯ	rua	ቷ	tua	ዯ	yua	ዷ	zua
ሷ	sua	ኟ	cua	ዿ	dua	ፏ	fua

TURKISH.

The Turkish language is a compound of words taken from the Tatar, Persian and Arabic languages. The high dialect, only spoken at Constantinople by people of quality, and serving as the written language, is a compound of Persian and Arabic words. Like most oriental languages, Turkish is written and read from right to left.

ا *Elif* supplies the german vowels *a*, *y*, *o*, *u*, the consonants of the word being hard; but the german *e*, *i*, *ö*, *ü*, the consonants being soft. When Alif is followed by a hard consonant, the ﹷ (*Ustun*) is pronounced like *a*, the ﹻ (*Esre*) like *y*, and the ﹹ (*Utru*) like *o* or *u*. Following, however, a soft consonant, the ﹷ (*Ustun*) is to be read as *e*, the ﹻ (*Esre*) as *i*, and the ﹹ (*Utru*) as *o* or *u*. In the middle and at the end of words, without Hamzalif, the Alif is always pronounced like *a*, but with Hamzalif, like *ê*.

ب *Ba* is our *b*. After *Ta*, *Tha*, *Jim*, *Cha*, *Sin*, *Shin*, *Ssad*, *Tta'*, *Qaf*, *Gef* it is often read like *p*.

پ *Pa* is our *p*.

ت *Ta* is our *t*. In the conjugation of some verbs it is changed into *Dal*.

ث *Tha* is our *s* or *ss*, except the word ثلث *tult*. The Arabs pronounce it like *th*.

ج *Jim*, the italian *g* before *e* or *i*. When meeting the consonants named above in connection with the letter ب, it is pronounced like *Tchim*.

چ *Tchin* like our *ch* in chess.

ح *Hha* like *h* in have.

خ *Cha*, the german *ch* in brauchen.

د *Dal* like *d*. It is pronounced like *t* when meeting the consonants named above in connection with the letter ب.

ذ *Dhal* like *z*.

ر *Ra* like *r*.

ز *Za* like our *z*.

س *Sin* like *s*, *ss*.

ش *Shin* like *sh*.

ص *Ssad* like sharp *ss*.

ض *Ddad*, like our *z*; the Arabs pronounce it like *d*.

ط *Tta* like *t* or *th*; it is often confounded with *Ta* and *Dal*.

ظ *Zza* like our *z*.

ع *Ain* like a strong guttural and nasal *a*, *y*, *u*.

غ *Ghain* like *g* guttural.

ف *Fa* like our *f*.

ق *Qaf* like *k*, *kh* or *ck*.

ك *Kaf*, like *q* or *k*, as in the french words *qui*, *quel*.

گ *Gef*, accords with our *g* in give; in some cases it is pronounced like *gi* very soft; in the middle of words and in some terminations like *y*.

ڭ *Saghur Nun*, i. e. mute Nun, like the french nasal-*n* in *mon*, *son*.

ل *Lam* our *l*; in some cases it is soft like *l* in limb, in some hard like *l* in all.

م *Mim*, like *m*.

ن *Nun* our *n*; but when followed by a *Ba*, it is pronounced like *m*.

و *Waw* our *w* or *v*; furnished with Utru, it is pronounced like *u* in conjunction with hard consonants; like german *ü* or *ö*, however, in conjunction with soft ones.

ه *Ha* like our *h*; at the end of words it is mostly pronounced like *a* or *e*.

لا *Lamelif*, *la* or *lia* (Ligature).

ى *Ya*, when a consonant like our *y*, when a vowel like *i*; it represents a vowel only in the middle or at the end of words.

ORTHOGRAPHICAL SIGNS.

ﹷ *Ustun* is placed over the consonants and pronounced like *a* with a hard consonant, like *e* with a soft one.

ﹻ *Esre* below the consonants, is pronounced like vowel *y* with a hard consonant, but like *i* with a soft one.

ﹹ *Utru* is pronounced like *o* or *u* with a hard consonant, but like *o* or *u* with a soft one.

ﹽ *Iki ustun* (double Ustun) like *en*.

ﹺ *Iki esre* (double Esre) like *in*.

ﹾ *Iki utru* (double Utru) like *on* or *un*.

The three last marks are only employed in Arabic words.

ﹿ *Jesm* (sign of pause) is placed over a consonant wanting a vowel, followed by an other consonant.

ﹳ *Teshdid* or *Shedde* when placed over a consonant doubles it.

ﹶ *Meddelif* or *Medda*, is only placed over the Alif, which, then, is always pronounced like *a*.

ﺀ *Hamzelif* or *Hamza*; placed over Elif, is pronounced like *ê*; over Waw, like *u*, over Ya, like *i*; at the end of words, ending with a vowel, like *i*.

PERSIAN

Name	Form				Pronun-ciation	Numer: value	Notes
	uncon-nected	connected with a preceding letter	connected with both	connected with a following letter			
Elif	ا	ل	.	.	Spiritus lenis	1	
Ba	ب	ب	٨	ﺑ	b	2	
Pa	پ	پ	٠	ﭘ	p	. . .	
Ta	ت	ت	٪	ﺗ	t soft	400	
Tha	ث	ث	ﺛ	ﺛ	s sharp	500	
Jim	ج	ج	ﺠ	ﺟ	j	3	
Tchim	چ	چ	ﭻ	ﭼ	tch	. . .	
Hha	ح	ح	ﺤ	ﺣ	hh sharp	8	
Cha	خ	خ	ﺨ	ﺧ	kh guttur.	600	
Dal	د	ﺪ	.	,	d	4	
Dhal	ذ	ﺬ			z soft	700	
Ra	ر	ﺮ			r	200	
Za	ز	ﺰ	.		z soft	7	
Zha	ژ	ﮋ			zh or j french	. . .	
Sin	س	س	ﺴ	ﺳ	s sharp	60	
Shin	ش	ش	ﺸ	ﺷ	sh	300	
Ssad	ص	ص	ﺼ	ﺻ	s sharp	90	
Ddad	ض	ض	ﻀ	ﺿ	z hard	800	
Tta	ط	ط	ﻄ	ﻃ	t	9	
Zza	ظ	ظ	ﻈ	ﻇ	z hard	900	
Ain	ع	ع	ﻌ	ﻋ	Spiritus lenis	70	
Ghain	غ	غ	ﻐ	ﻏ	gh guttur.	1000	
Fa	ف	ف	ﻔ	ﻓ	f	80	
Qaf	ق	ق	ﻘ	ﻗ	k guttur.	100	
Kaf	ک	ك	ﻜ	ﻛ	k	20	
Gaf	گ	ﮓ	ﮕ	ﮔ	g palatal	. . .	
Lam	ل	ل	ﻠ	ﻟ	l	30	
Mim	م	م	ﻤ	ﻣ	m	40	
Nun	ن	ن	ﻨ	ﻧ	n	50	
Waw	و	ﻮ			w	6	
Ha	ه	ﺨ	ﻬ	ﻫ	h	5	
Ya	ی	ی	ﻴ	ﻳ	y and i	10	

Notes

Many Arabic words having been introduced into the Persian language, the Persian alphabet consists of 32 consonants, which are written and read from right to left; of these consonants, 28 are common to both languages; only the following four are purely Persian:

پ چ ژ گ

VOWELS.

All Persian letters are consonants, except Elif, Waw and Ya, which also supply long vowels (the Waw, sometimes, represents a short vowel):

ا a و w ی y

The short vowels are written thus:

ـَ Zabar, a ـِ Zir, e ـُ Pish, u

ORTHOGRAPHICAL SIGNS.

ء Hamza, at the end of a word, sometimes supplies the Elif; it is also placed above an Elif in the middle of a word, when the Elif represents a consonant.

ـّ Teshdid, doubles the letter over which it is placed.

ـٓ Medda. Instead of an Elif written twice, a Medda is placed over it. It is properly a second Elif, but written lengthwise; sometimes it has a vertical form.

ـْ Jezma, over a consonant by which a syllable ends. It is also placed over Waw or Ya, when they form a diphthong with a preceding.

CIPHERS.

To write numbers, the Persians employ either the alphabet, or the Arabic ciphers (see under).

LIGATURE.

لا لا Lam-Elif, la.

4*

AFGHAN OR PUSHTOO

| Figure | | | Pronun- | Figure | | | Pronun- |
unconnected	in the midst	at the com-mencement	ciation	unconnected	in the midst	at the com-mencement	ciation
‍ا	‍ا ‍ل	‍ا	a, á, i, u	ش	‍ش	ش	sh
ب	‍ب	‍ب	b	ڼ	‍ڼ	‍ڼ	khíu
پ	‍پ	‍پ	p	ص	‍ص	ص	ss
ت	‍ت	‍ت	t	ض	‍ض	ض	dz
ټ	‍ټ	‍ټ	tt	ط	‍ط	ط	t
ث	‍ث	‍ث	t's	ظ	‍ظ	ظ	z
څ	‍څ	‍څ	t's	ع	‍ع	‍ع	æ, á
ج	‍ج	‍ج	j	غ	‍غ	‍غ	gh
چ	‍چ	‍چ	ch	ف	‍ف	ف	f
ح	‍ح	‍ح	h	ق	‍ق	ق	k, q
خ	‍خ	‍خ	kh	ک	‍ک	‍ک	k
د	‍د	د	d	گ	‍گ	گ	g
ډ	‍ډ	ډ	dd	ل	‍ل	ل	l
ذ	‍ذ	ذ	z	م	‍م	م	m
ر	‍ر	ر	r	ن	‍ن	ن	n
ړ	‍ړ	ړ	rr	ڼ	‍ڼ	ڼ	rrn
ز	‍ز	ز	z	و	‍و	و	w ú o
ژ	‍ژ	ژ	dz	ه	‍ه	ه	h
ژ ر	‍ژ ‍ژ	ژ ژ	jz	ه	‍ه	ه	a
س	‍س	‍س	s	ی	‍ی	ی	y, e, í, ai

NOTES.

Before the introduction of arabic words, the original Pushtoo alphabet consisted only of 29 different sounds; at present, the Afghans make use also of the 28 arabic letters, and of these four letters used in Persian: پ چ ژ and گ, from which results an alphabet of 40 different characters which are all consonants.

The Pushtoo vowels are the same as the Arabic and Persian:

‍ٔ Zabar or Fatha a, ‍ٔ Zer or Kasrah e, ‍ٔ Pesh or Zammah u.

They are placed either above or under the consonant beginning a syllable, as: بَ ba, بِ bi, بُ bu. Zabar followed by ‍ٔ is read as the

diphthong au; followed by ی, as the diphthong ai.

‍ٔ or ‍ٔ Jesm or Jesmah indicates that the consonant has no vowel and the syllable is finished.

‍ٓ Meddah or Medd, an other form of Elif, is sign of producing a syllable.

‍ٔ Teshdid indicates that a consonant is to be pronounced double.

‍ٔ Weslu, joining-mark.

‍ٔ Hamzah supplies the place of Elif.

‍ٔ ‍ٔ ‍ٔ Tanwin is the arabic Nunation at the end of the words, pronounced by adding a n to the vowels: an, in, yn.

COPTIC

Figure		Name	Pronunciation	Notes
Ⲁ	ⲁ	Alpha	ă	The Coptic language is divided into two dialects: the upper-egyptian or thebaic or sahidic, and the lower-egyptian or memphitic or coptic par excellence, to which may be added a third, the bashmuric dialect. The letters ⲁ — ⲱ in the Coptic alphabet are of greek origin; ϥ — ϭ on the other hand signify sounds which either wanted at all in the greek language, or which since the christian era no longer used in writing; they are taken from the older egyptian. This sign ϯ denotes the syllable ti: its prototype is the semitic and greek Tau. The vowels are:
Ⲃ	ⲃ	Vida	b v	
Ⲅ	ⲅ	Gamma	g	
Ⲇ	ⲇ	Dalda	d	
Ⲉ	ⲉ	Ei	ĕ	
Ⲍ	ⲍ	Zida	z	
Ⲏ	ⲏ	Hida	ī	
Ⲑ	ⲑ	Thida	th	
Ⲓ	ⲓ	Jauda	ī	ⲁ ⲉ ⲓ ⲟ,
Ⲕ	ⲕ	Kabba	k	the oo is written by ⲟⲩ, like in greek; before a consonant it is pronounced by oo, before a vowel by v. The coptic diphthongs are:
Ⲗ	ⲗ	Laula	l	
Ⲙ	ⲙ	Mi	m	
Ⲛ	ⲛ	Ni	n	ⲁⲓ ⲉⲓ ⲟⲓ
Ⲝ	ⲝ	Exi	x	pronounced in the sahidic dialect only as ĕ, ī, ī, in the memphitic, however, as the german diphthongs ai, ei, oi.
Ⲟ	ⲟ	O	o short	
Ⲡ	ⲡ	Pi	p b	**READING - SIGNS AND PUNCTUATION.**
Ⲣ	ⲣ	Ro	r	ˈ above a letter: the greek gravis.
Ⲥ	ⲥ	Sima	s	ˈ behind a word in sahidic manuscripts: dividing sign.
Ⲧ	ⲧ	Dau	t d	•ʃ signifies a greater pause, like our semicolon or point.
Ⲩ	ⲩ	He	i, ü Germ.	⁚ signifies a shorter pause, like our comma.
Ⲫ	ⲫ	Phi	ph	— sign of division.
Ⲭ	ⲭ	Chi	ch sc	⎯ sign of abbreviature above the characters.
Ⲯ	ⲯ	Ebsi	ps	⌒ graphic sign above some characters in sahidic manuscripts.
Ⲱ	ⲱ	O	o long	ˈ diacritic sign behind some words in sahidic manuscripts.
Ϥ	ϥ	Fei	f ph	, Comma, only in later sahidic manuscripts.
Ϩ	ϩ	Hori	h	• orthographic sign above some characters in memphitic books.
Ϧ	ϧ	Chei	kh	
Ϣ	ϣ	Scei	sh	
Ϫ	ϫ	Giangia	g dsh	**NUMERICAL VALUE.**
Ϭ	ϭ	Scima	sk sc gh	The numerical value of the coptic characters is the same as in greek. Numerals are written by ⎯ above the letters; the thousands are marked by , below near the letter. ϥ (90) supplies the place of the greek ϙ (koppa).
ϯ	ϯ	Dei Ligature	ti	
Ϛ	ϛ	So	Cipher 6	

CHINESE.

A calculation, based upon the Imperial Chinese Dictionary, shows that the Chinese language is represented by 43,496 characters or symbols. Of this number 13,000 are totally irrelevant and consist of signs which are obsolete, incorrectly formed, and unexplained. For the expressions in ordinary literature about 4000 signs appear to suffice. The writings of Con-foo-tse (Confucius) and his disciples can even be read by the help of only 2500 characters, and a knowledge of these will enable the student tolerably to understand all Chinese works on history and philosophy. In lieu of the phonetic and lexicographical system, which appertains to most languages, the Chinese have adopted 214 signs any of which, being placed by the side of an unknown character, indicates at once its pronunciation. These indicators of sound, are termed by the Chinese "Tribunals". European grammarians have called them "Keys" or "Radicals". Occasionally the "Tones" (modulating accents) are appended at the top or foot of the character, at the right or the left side. Such accents are described as follows,

1 ⃞。 even tone. 2 ⃞。 entering tone. 3 ⃞° falling tone. 4 °⃞ rising tone.

The "Keys" are divided into 17 Classes, according to the number of strokes of which each character is composed, and are arranged in the following order:

Class					Class					
1. consisting of 1 stroke extends from Nr.	1—6				10. consisting of 10 strokes extends from Nr.187—194					
2.	"	" 2 strokes	"	" " 7—29	11.	"	" 11 "	"	" " 195—200	
3.	"	" 3 "	"	" " 30—60	12.	"	" 12 "	"	" " 201—204	
4.	"	" 4 "	"	" " 61—94	13.	"	" 13 "	"	" " 205—208	
5.	"	" 5 "	"	" " 95—117	14.	"	" 14 "	"	" " 209—210	
6.	"	" 6 "	"	" " 118—146	15.	"	" 15 "	"	" " 211	
7.	"	" 7 "	"	" " 147—166	16.	"	" 16 "	"	" " 212—213	
8.	"	" 8 "	"	" " 167—175	17.	"	" 17 "	"	" " 214	
9.	"	" 9 "	"	" " 176—186						

1	一。	yĭ, one	17	凵。	kăn	33	士。	s'z, scholar
2	丨。	chiĕh, perpendicular stroke	18	刀	tou, knife	34	又°	fanfun
3	丶。	tien, point	19	力	liĕ, strength	35	夊°	tsieh, slowly
4	丿。	piĕh, stroke slanting to the left	20	勹	chwen, equal, triangle	36	夕°	dsiĕh, evening
5	乙。	yi, crooked stroke	21。	匕	pi, spoon	37。	大	tá, great
6	亅。	kiu, hooked stroke	22	匚	fang, to pull out	38	女°	nü, girl
7。	二	urh, two	23	匸。	kwah, division between fields	39	子°	tsĕ, son, child
8。	亠	yitièn-yiwa	24	十	shiàh, ten	40。	宀	mou or poën-an hat
9	人。	jin, man	25	卜°	poh, to divine	41	寸	tsun, inch
10	儿	chàh, foot	26	卩°	tsshi	42°	小	siou, small
11	入。	shàh, to enter	27	厂°	shi, shelter	43	尢。	kang, horrible
12	八。	pah, eight	28	厶°	chee, perverse	44	尸°	shi, corpse
13	冂。	kwah, desert	29	又°	yiu, again, moreover	45	屮°	tsou
14。	宀	mièn, to cover	30	口。	kiu, mouth	46	山°	san, mountain
15°	冫	pin, ice	31°	囗	hwei, return	47。	巛	chuĕn, stream
16	几°	chi, bench	32。	土	too, the ground	48°	工	kòng, artisan, time

49	已	*chi,* self	73	曰	*yuěh,* to talk	97	瓜 *kwah,* melon
50	巾	*chin,* cloth	74	月	*yueh,* moon	98	瓦 *wàh,* tiles, earthenware
51	干	*kan,* shield, spear	75	木	*moh,* tree	99	甘 *kan,* sweet
52	幺	*yuěn,* source	76	欠	*chièn,* debtor	100	生 *senn,* to live, to give birth
53	广	*yin,* hut	77	止	*ts',* to stop	101	用 *yòng,* to use
54	廴	*tsou,* long walk	78	歹	*tie,* wicked	102	田 *tièn,* field
55	廾	*kòng,* higher	79	殳	*kòh,* the young of animals	103	疋 *pièh,* piece
56	弋	*yièh,* spear	80	毋	*f'ò,* is not	104	疒 *tsièh,* sick
57	弓	*kòng,* a bow	81	比	*pi,* to compare	105	癶 *fàh,* to divide
58	彐	*kway,* Come!	82	毛	*mou,* feather	106	白 *buh,* white
59	彡	*san,* coat	83	氏	*sz,* clan	107	皮 *bi,* skin
60	彳	*shuang-jiu,* two men	84	气	*chi,* air	108	皿 *min,* implement
61	心	*sin,* heart	85	水	*shway,* water	109	目 *mòh,* eye
62	戈	*kòh,* a lance	86	火	*chaw,* fire	110	矛 *maòh,* spear
63	戶	*w'òo,* inner door	87	爪	*tsou,* claws, nails	111	矢 *shi,* arrow
64	手	*sheu,* hand	88	父	*f'òh,* father	112	石 *shièh,* stone
65	支	*tz',* branch	89	爻	*yow,* sign	113	示 *sz,* to admonish
66	攴	*chi,* the stalk	90	爿	*chwang,* pole	114	肉 *nahy or shòh,* clapper of a bell
67	文	*funn,* gentle	91	片	*pièn,* splinter	115	禾 *haw,* grain
68	斗	*tou,* a measure	92	牙	*yah,* teeth	116	穴 *yuěh,* cave
69	斤	*chin,* hatchet, pound	93	牛	*niu,* ox	117	立 *lìè,* to stand
70	方	*fang,* a square, then	94	犬	*chuèn,* dog	118	竹 *choh,* bamboo
71	无	*f'è,* no	95	玄	*yuěn,* interminable	119	米 *mi,* rice
72	日	*shèh,* sun, day	96	玉	*nièh,* gem	120	糸 *s'z,* silk

121	缶	f'ow, jar	145	衣	i, clothing
122	网	kang, hedge	146	西	yiu, twilight
123	羊	yang, sheep	147	見	chièn, to see
124	羽	ü, long feathers	148	角	krìh, horn, corner
125	老	laò, old	149	言	nièn, word
126	而	urh, and	150	谷	kòh, apertures in rocks
127	耒	lie, handle of a spade	151	豆	tou, head
128	耳	ull, the ear	152	豕	shü, swine
129	聿	yuĕh, to manifest, a baton	153	豸	chi, superior order of animals
130	肉	jòh, flesh	154	貝	pèi, valuables
131	臣	chin, an official	155	赤	chĕh, red
132	自	ts'z, from oneself	156	走	tsou, to walk
133	至	tsz, to arrive, extreme	157	足	tsòh, leg
134	臼	chiu, mortar	158	身	shin, body
135	舌	chweh, tongue	159	車	chü, cart
136	舛	chiah, strong	160	辛	sin, bitter, hardships
137	舟	chiu, vessel	161	辰	jĕn, an hour, azure
138	艮	kun, inferior order of nature	162	辵	tseu, to run
139	色	sĕh, colour	163	邑	jĕ, a town
140	艸	tsaò, grass	164	酉	yoo, twilight
141	虍	'hoo, tiger	165	釆	tsie, to separate
142	虫	chŏng, insects	166	里	li, one third of a mile
143	血	shwĕh, blood	167	金	chin, gold, metal
144	行	jĕn, to walk, to act	168	長	chang, long

169	門	mun, a door
170	阜	fou, a mound
171	隶	di, to accomplish
172	隹	chiah, fine
173	雨	yü, rain
174	青	tsin, green
175	非	feeh, not
176	面	mièn, face
177	革	kĕh, leather
178	韋	hway, high
179	韭	chiu, leeks
180	音	yin, a sound, tone
181	頁	hièh, a sheet, a leaf
182	風	fong, wind
183	飛	fee, to fly
184	食	shĕh, to eat
185	首	sheu, head
186	香	shiang, scent
187	馬	máa, horse
188	骨	kwĭh, bones
189	高	kaò, high
190	髟	kaò, whiskers, beard
191	鬥	tou, to fight
192	鬯	chang, sweet wine

193 鬲 *lièh*, to cup open	201 黃 *hwang*, yellow	208 鼠 *chü*, rat
194 鬼 *kway*, devil	202 黍 *shü*, millet	209 鼻 *pièh*, nose
195 魚 *nü*, fish	203 黑 *'hĕh*, black	210 齊 *tsi*, to put in order, equal
196 鳥 *niaò*, bird	204 黹 *chi*, embroidery	211 齒 *ts'z*, the back teeth
197 鹵 *loo*, brine	205 黽 *min*, a toad	212 龍 *long*, dragon
198 鹿 *lòh*, stag	206 鼎 *tin*, tripod	213 龜 *kway*, tortoise
199 麥 *mèh*, wheat	207 鼓 *koo*, drum	214 龠 *yàh*, a musical instrument
200 麻 *má*, hemp		

ARITHMETICAL FIGURES.

All arithmetical combinations are performed by 17 Cardinal figures. In the subjoined table, three different forms of numerical characters are given. The series in the left column represents the *plain hand* which serves for literary and ordinary purposes. In the middle column *words* are employed instead of figures. This class is used in bonds, contracts etc., where it is of importance to guard against alterations and fraud. The figures in the right column, written in a "running hand", are used by merchants and traders in keeping their business accounts.

一	壹	〡	*yĕ*,	1
二	貳	〢	*urh*,	2
三	叄	〣	*san*,	3
四	肆	〤	*s'z*,	4
五	伍	〥	*oo*,	5
六	陸	〦	*loh*,	6
七	柒	〧	*tsiĕ*,	7
八	捌	〨	*pàh*,	8
九	玖	〩	*cheu*,	9
十	拾	十	*shiàh*.	10
百		百	*pĕh*,	100
千		千	*tsièn*,	1000
萬		万	*van*,	10,000
億		億	*ee*,	100,000
兆		兆	*chaò*,	1,000,000
京		京	*chin*,	10,000,000
垓		垓	*nyàh*,	100,000,000

The numbers by which 10, 100 etc. are multiplied are placed at the top of the multiplicand. The numbers added to ten etc., are marked below the figure.

Example 十 ten. 二十二 twice ten and two, or 22.

JAPANESE
IN THE KATA-KANA CHARACTER.
(This type was cut under the direction of Prof. J. HOFFMAN of Leyden and cast by N. TETTERODE in Rotterdam.)

I-RO-FA (Abc).				THE JAPANESE ALPHABET organically arranged. *					
25 井 yi		1 イ i		1 ア a		25 セ se		49 バ ba	
26 ノ no		2 ロ ro		2 ワ wa		26 ゼ ze		50 パ pa	
27 オ o		3 ハ fa, va		3 エ e		27 シ si		51 ヘ fe	
28 ク ku		4 ニ ni		4 イ i		28 ジ zi		52 ベ be	
29 ヤ ya		5 ホ fo		5 オ o		29 ソ so		53 ペ pe	
30 マ ma		6 ヘ fe, ve		6 ヲ wo		30 ゾ zo		54 ビ fi	
31 ケ ke		7 ト to		7 ウ u		31 ス su		55 ビ bi	
32 ン fu		8 チ tsi		8 ヤ ya		32 ズ zu		56 ピ pi	
33 コ ko		9 リ ri		9 エ ye		33 タ ta		57 ホ fo	
34 エ ye		10 ヌ nu		10 井 yi		34 ダ da		58 ボ bo	
35 テ te		11 ル ru		11 ヨ yo		35 テ te		59 ポ po	
36 ア a		12 ヲ wo		12 ユ yu		36 デ de		60 ン fu	
37 サ sa		13 ワ wa		13 カ ka		37 チ tsi		61 ブ bu	
38 キ ki		14 カ ka		14 ガ ga		38 ヂ dsi		62 プ pu	
39 ユ yu		15 ヨ yo		15 ケ ke		39 ト to		63 ナ na	
40 メ me		16 ダ da		16 ゲ ge		40 ド do		64 子 ne	
41 ミ mi		17 レ re		17 キ ki		41 ツ tsu		65 ニ ni	
42 シ si		18 ン so		18 ギ gi		42 ヅ dsu		66 ノ no	
43 エ e		19 ツ tsu		19 コ ko		43 マ ma		67 ヌ nu	
44 ヒ fi, vi		20 子 ne		20 ゴ go		44 メ me		68 ン n	
45 モ mo		21 ナ na		21 ク ku		45 ミ mi		69 ラ ra	
46 セ se		22 ラ ra		22 グ gu		46 モ mo		70 レ re	
47 ス su		23 ム mu		23 サ sa		47 ム mu		71 リ ri	
		24 ウ u		24 ザ za		48 ハ fa		72 ロ ro	
								73 ル ru	

* The accent *niguri*, consisting of two minute marks at the right of the syllable, softens the consonant. The accent *mark*, a dot likewise at the right, hardens the consonant. By the addition of those marks and the n, unattended by a vowel, the letters originally 47, are raised to the number of 73.

ABBREVIATIONS AND ORTHOGRAPHICAL SIGNS.

コ koto. ゴ goto. ノ site. 王 tama.

ヽ Sign of doubling a letter, placed in the middle line.

〱 Sign of doubling a syllable.

〉 Sign of lengthening a vowel.

' Full stop. ヽ comma, towards the right, beyond the middle line.

SANSCRIT

CONSONANTS.

Each consonant is sounded with an inherent short *a*.

GUTTURALS.		LABIALS.	
क	ka	प	pa
ख	kha	फ	pha
ग	ga	ब	ba
घ	gha	भ	bha
ङ	ṅa	म	ma

PALATALS.		SEMI-VOWELS.	
च	cha	य	ya
छ	ch'ha	र	ra
ज	ja	ल	la
झ	j'ha	व	va
ञ	ña		

CEREBRALS.		SIBILANTS AND ASPIRATES.	
ट	ṭa	श	sha
ठ	ṭha	ष	sh'ha
ड	ḍa	स	sa
ढ	ḍha	ह	ha
ण	ṇa		

DENTALS.	
त	ta
थ	tha
द	da
ध	dha
न	na

ऴ ḻ

This character peculiar to the Rig-Veda has a sound which partakes of *l* and *r*. It stands for the cerebral *ḍa*. When it represents the aspirate of this letter, it is expressed by ऴ (*ḻha*).

VOWELS.

The vowels in the left row are uttered as initials or are placed before their consonants. The vowel-signs in the right division being medials and finals, coalesce with their consonants, and are respectively placed over, under, before and after the letters.

अ	a		COALESCENT VOWELS.
आ	â	ा â	follows the consonant
इ	i	ि i	precedes „
ई	î	ी î	follows „
उ	u	ु u	under
ऊ	û	ू û	„ „
ऋ	r̤	ृ r̤	„ „
ॠ	r̤̂	ॄ r̤̂	„ „
ऌ	l̤	ॢ l̤	„ „
		ॣ l̤	„ „

DIPHTHONGS.

ए	e	े e	over „
ऐ	ai	ै ai	„ „
ओ	o	ो o	follows „
औ	au	ौ au	„ „

NASAL SOUNDS.

ं Anusvâra and ँ Anunâsika, are substitutes for *m* and *n*. The anunâsika has its place above the letter or laterally with virâma underneath.

ः ḥ (or properly ख़ः) visarga, + jihvâmûlîya and × upadhmânîya, are strong final aspirates. The visarga which is the substitute for *s* and *r* is the only one in common use. The last two signs bear also the common designation of ardhavisarga.

ADDITIONAL SIGNS.

˘ *Virâma* (pause) is placed under a final consonant, and denotes the absence of the inherent short *a*.

। indicates the close of a sentence, ending in a vowel, a diphthong or a visarga. In poetry it denotes the half of a verse. At the end of a verse or a period this mark is doubled ॥.

ऽ serves 1. as the sign of hiatus, 2. as sign of the elision of *a* after *e* and *o*, 3. as the sign of coalescence of two *a*.

० is the sign of abbreviation.

ऱ and ऱ represent the letter *r*. The former sign is pronounced before the consonant (and the semivowel ri) at the top of which it is placed; the latter sign is placed under the consonant and sounded after it.

PROSODIAL MARKS.

⏑ denotes brevity, ⏤ length.

ACCENTS.

˳ *Anudâtta* or grave accent stands under the vowel.

˴ *Swarita* or circumflex is put over the vowel.

In connexion with these marks the numerals ९ and ३ serve as accents.

NUMERALS.

१	२	३	४	५	६	७	८	९	०
1	2	3	4	5	6	7	8	9	0

SANSCRIT

The similarity of shape occasions mistakes in correcting proofs; it may therefore be of advantage both to compositors and readers of proofs to make use of the annexed numbers of reference. The form of the subjoined Alphabet differs from that which precedes, but is superior in point of correctness.

1	अ	a	27	ॆ॑	re(with Acc.)	53	क्य	kya	79	ङ्क	ṅka
2	आ	â	28	ै॑	ai(with Acc.)	54	क्र	kra	80	ङ्क्त	ṅkta
3	इ	i	29	ैँ	raim̐	55	क्र	kra	81	ङ्क्य	ṅkya
4	ई	î	30	ः	Accents and other orthographical signs.	56	क्ल	kla	82	ङ्क्ष	ṅksha
5	उ	u	31	ं		57	क्व	kva	83	ङ्ख	ṅkha
6	ऊ	û	32	ँ		58	क्ष	ksha (x)	84	ङ्ख्य	ṅkhya
7	ऋ	ṛi	33	।		59	क्ष्	ksh	85	ङ्ग	ṅga
8	ॠ	ṛ̂i	34	॥		60	क्ष्म	kshma	86	ङ्ग्य	ṅgya
9	ऌ	ḷi	35	॰		61	क्ष्य	kshya	87	ङ्घ	ṅgha
10	ॡ	ḷ̂i	36	-		62	क्ष्व	kshva	88	ङ्घ्य	ṅghya
11	ए	e	37	ऽ		63	ख	kha	89	ङ्घ्र	ṅghra
12	ा	â	38	×		64	ख्	kh	90	ङ्ङ	ṅṅa
13	ि	i	39	ˎ		65	ख्य	khya	91	च	cha (ća)
14	ी	î	40	ˆ		66	ग	ga	92	च्	ch (ć)
15	ीँ	rî	41	–		67	ग्	g	93	च्च	ćća
16	ु	u	42	।		68	ग्न	gna	94	च्छ	ććha
17	ू	û	43	ॅ		69	ग्न्य	gnya	95	च्ञ	ćña
18	ृ	ṛi	44	ॎ		70	ग्र	gra	96	च्म	ćma
19	ॄ	ṛ̂i	45	॒		71	ग्र्य	grya	97	च्य	ćya
20	ॢ	ḷi	46	क	ka	72	घ	gha	98	छ	ćha
21	ॣ	ḷ̂i	47	क्क	kka	73	घ्	gh	99	छ्र	ćhra
22	े	e	48	क्त	kta	74	घ्न	ghna	100	ज	ja
23	ै	ai	49	क्त्य	ktya	75	घ्म	ghma	101	ज्	j
24	ो	o	50	क्त्व	ktva	76	घ्य	ghya	102	ज्ज	jja
25	े॑	e(with Acc.)	51	क्न	kna	77	घ्र	ghra	103	ज्ञ	jña
26	ॆ	re	52	क्म	kma	78	ङ	ṅa	104	ज्ञ्	jñ

SANSCRIT

105	ऋ	jjha	133	राङ	ṇḍra	161	थ	th	189	ध्य	dhya
106	ज्य	jya	134	राञ्झ	ṇḍrya	162	थ्य	thya	190	ध्र	dhra
107	ज्र	jra	135	राढ	ṇḍha	163	द	da	191	ध्व	dhva
108	ज्व	jva	136	ष्ण	ṇṇa	164	दु	du	192	न	na
109	फ	jha	137	राय	ṇya	165	दू	dú	193	ऽ	n
110	भ्र	jha	138	राब	ṇva	166	ह	dṛi	194	न्त	nta
111	ञ	ña	139	त	ta	167	झ	dga	195	न्य	ntya
112	ङ	ñ	140	ғ	t	168	ङ	dgha	196	न्त्र	ntra
113	ञ्च	ñća	141	त्क	tka	169	ह्	dda	197	न्द	nda
114	ञ्ज	ñja	142	त्त	tta	170	ड्ब	ddba	198	न्द्र	ndra
115	ट	ṭa	143	त्य	ttya	171	ह्य	ddya	199	न्थ	ndha
116	द्क	ṭka	144	त्ल	ttra	172	ड्ड	ddha	200	न्ध्र	ndhra
117	ट्	ṭṭa	145	ख	ttva	173	ड्झ	ddhya	201	न्न	nna
118	ट्य	ṭya	146	त्न	tna	174	न	dna	202	न्र	npra
119	ठ	ṭha	147	त्प	tpa	175	ड्ब	dba	203	न्फ	npha
120	ठ्य	ṭhya	148	त्म	tpra	176	ड्र	dbra	204	क्र	nphra
121	ठ्	ṭhra	149	त्फ	tpha	177	झ	dbha	205	न्म	nma
122	ड	ḍa	150	त्फ्र	tphra	178	झ्झ	dbhya	206	न्य	nya
123	ड्ड	ḍḍa	151	त्म	tma	179	ड्र	dma	207	न्स	nsa
124	ड्ड	ḍḍa	152	त्म्य	tmya	180	ह्य	dya	208	प	pa
125	ढ	ḍha	153	त्य	tya	181	द्र	dra	209	ऽ	p
126	ढ्य	ḍhya	154	च	tra	182	द्द्य	drya	210	प्त	pta
127	ढ्	ḍhra	155	च्य	trya	183	द्व	dva	211	प्न	pna
128	ण	ṇa	156	त्व	tva	184	द्व्य	dvya	212	प्प	ppa
129	ण्	ṇ	157	त्स	tsa	185	ध	dha	213	प्म	pma
130	राट	ṇṭa	158	त्स्न	tsna	186	६	dh	214	प्य	pya
131	राठ	ṇṭha	159	त्स्य	tsya	187	भ्र	dhna	215	प्र	pra
132	राड	ṇḍa	160	थ	tha	188	ध्म	dhma	216	प्ल	pla

№			№			№			№		
217	प्व	pva	245	य	ya	273	श्र	çra	301	स	sma
218	प्स	psa	246	र	y	274	श्ल	çla	302	स्म्य	smya
219	फ	pha	247	च	y	275	श्व	çva	303	स्य	sya
220	ब	ba	248	य्य	yya	276	श्श	çça	304	स्र	sra
221	ड	b	249	र	ra	277	ष	sha	305	स्व	sva
222	ब्घ	bgha	250	रु	ru	278	ष	sh	306	स्स	ssa
223	ब्ज	bja	251	रू	rû	279	ष्ट	shṭa	307	ह	ha
224	ब्द	bda	252	ल	la	280	ष्ट्य	shṭya	308	ह	h
225	ब्ध	bdha	253	ल	l	281	ष्ट्र	shṭra	309	हृ	hṛi
226	ब्ब	bba	254	ल्क	lka	282	ष्ट्र्य	shṭrya	310	ह्ण	hṇa
227	ब्भ	bbha	255	ल्प	lpa	283	ष्ट्र्य	shṭrya	311	ह्न	hna
228	ब्र	bra	256	ल्म	lma	284	ष्ट्व	shṭva	312	ह्म	hma
229	भ	bha	257	ल्य	lya	285	ष्ठ	shṭha	313	ह्य	hya
230	भ	bh	258	ल्ल	lla	286	ष्ण	shṇa	314	ह्र	hra
231	भ्य	bhya	259	ल्व	lva	287	ष्प	shpa	315	ह्ल	hla
232	भ्र	bhra	260	व	va	288	ष्प्र	shpra	316	ह्व	hva
233	भ्व	bhva	261	व	v	289	ष्म	shma	317	ळ	ḻ
234	म	ma	262	व	v	290	ष्य	shya	318	ळ्ह	ḻha
235	म	m	263	व्य	vya	291	स	sa	319	१	1
236	म्न	mna	264	व्र	vra	292	स	s	320	२	2
237	म्प	mpa	265	व्व	vva	293	स्क	ska	321	३	3
238	म्प्र	mpra	266	श	ça	294	स्ख	skha	322	४	4
239	म्ब	mba	267	श	ça	295	स्त	sta	323	५	5
240	म्भ	mbha	268	श	ç	296	स्त्र	stra	324	६	6
241	म्य	mya	269	श	ç	297	स्थ	stha	325	७	7
242	म्र	mra	270	श्च	çéa	298	स्न	sna	326	८	8
243	म्ल	mla	271	श्च्य	ççya	299	स्प	spa	327	९	9
244	म्स	msa	272	श्न	çna	300	स्फ	spha	328	०	0

TAMIL

The Tamil language was earlier cultivated than the other members of the Drâvidian family. It includes two dialects the (ancient) *Shen-Tamil* and the (modern) *Kodun-Tamil*. Tamil is spoken throughout the plain of the Carnatic, below the ghauts from Pulicat to cape Comorin, to the neighbourhood of Trivandrum; also in the northern and western part of Ceylon where in ancient times Tamilians established their settlements. This language has 12 vowels and 18 consonants. It is read from left to right.

SHORT VOWELS.

அ	a	as in America
இ	i	" " fill
உ	u	" " full
எ	e	" " self
ஒ	o	" " long

THE CORRESPONDING LONG VOWELS.

ஆ	â	in ah
ஈ	î	" feel
ஊ	û	" foo
ஏ	ê	" they
ஓ	ô	" sole

DIPHTHONGS.

ஐ	ey	in eye
ஒள	ou	" foul

CONSONANTS.

க்	k	
ங்	n̈	ng in long
ச்	s	
ஞ்	ñ	as gn in french *régne*
ட்	ṭ	like t d of Sanscrit cerebrals
ண்	ṇ	like n of Sanscrit cerebral
த்	t	
ந்	n	in no
ப்	p	
ம்	m	
ற்	ṛ	rolled, partly like a cerebral, partly like a dental
ன்	ṅ	as in on

LIQUIDS.

ய்	y	as in yes
ர்	r	" " round
ல்	l	" " lap
வ்	v	
ள்	l	hard, it is of cerebral character
ழ்	l	intermediate between r and l.

The consonants have been divided into *rough*, *soft* and *intermediate* sounds. The first class includes the *tenues* (க், ச், ட், த், ப், ற்). The second class contains the corresponding Nasals. The third class contains the Liquids. A dot placed at the top of a consonant indicates the absence of a vowel, but is omitted in native MSS.

The following rules are to be noticed in the pronunciation.

a) Short *a*, before the soft letters ள், ண், the intermediate letters ர், ல், ள், ழ், and at the end of polysyllabic words, sounds like *e* in men.

b) Combined with a preceding *r* it receives the same sound.

c) The vowels *e* and *ê* as initials are pronounced as if *y* were placed before them.

d) The vowels *i* (*î*) and *e* (*ê*) before lingnals (ட், ண் and ள், ற் and ழ்) are respectively articulated somewhat deeper than the French *u* and *eu*.

e) The consonants க், த், ப் are only hardened as initial letters, or when doubled in the middle of a word. The same is the case with ட் which does not occur as an initial in pure Tamil words.

f) When க், ட், த், ப் occur as medials of a word, க் sounds like *ch*, ப் like *b*, த் like *th*, and ட் like the Sanscrit cerebral *d*.

g) ச் is always sharply hissed like *ss*. When the nasal ஞ் precedes, it coalesces with it and sounds like *ng* (in *angel*). When doubled after ட், or ற், it sounds like *ch* (in *church*).

h) *e* and *y* at the end of a syllable have an intermediate sound of *i* (in *vine*) and *ai* (in *rain*).

i) Double ற் sounds like *tt*. After the corresponding nasal ன், it may be pronounced like *d*.

The Tamil Alphabet being syllabic, a word is divisible in any part, so long as the consonant remains united with its vowel. In punctuation the full stop alone is employed.

The vowels, in their separate forms, are only used as initials. The following table shows their mode of coalition whith the consonants. The short *a*, as in Sanscrit, is not expressed before a consonant.

	a	â	i	î	u	û	e	ê	ey	o	ô	au
	அ	ஆ	இ	ஈ	உ	ஊ	எ	ஏ	ஐ	ஒ	ஓ	ஔ
k	க	கா	கி	கீ	கு	கூ	கெ	கே	கை	கொ	கோ	கௌ
ṅ	ங											
s	ச	சா	சி	சீ	சு	சூ	செ	சே	சை	சொ	சோ	சௌ
ñ	ஞ	ஞா	ஞி	ஞீ	ஞு	ஞூ	ஞெ	ஞே	ஞை	ஞொ	ஞோ	ஞௌ
ṭ	ட	டா	டி	டீ	டு	டூ	டெ	டே	டை	டொ	டோ	டௌ
ṇ	ண	ணா	ணி	ணீ	ணு	ணூ	ணெ	ணே	ணை	ணொ	ணோ	ணௌ
t	த	தா	தி	தீ	து	தூ	தெ	தே	தை	தொ	தோ	தௌ
ṅ	ந	நா	நி	நீ	நு	நூ	நெ	நே	நை	நொ	நோ	நௌ
p	ப	பா	பி	பீ	பு	பூ	பெ	பே	பை	பொ	போ	பௌ
m	ம	மா	மி	மீ	மு	மூ	மெ	மே	மை	மொ	மோ	மௌ
y	ய	யா	யி	யீ	யு	யூ	யெ	யே	யை	யொ	யோ	யௌ
r	ர	ரா	ரி	ரீ	ரு	ரூ	ரெ	ரே	ரை	ரொ	ரோ	ரௌ
l	ல	லா	லி	லீ	லு	லூ	லெ	லே	லை	லொ	லோ	லௌ
v	வ	வா	வி	வீ	வு	வூ	வெ	வே	வை	வொ	வோ	வௌ
ḷ	ழ	ழா	ழி	ழீ	ழு	ழூ	ழெ	ழே	ழை	ழொ	ழோ	ழௌ
l	ள	ளா	ளி	ளீ	ளு	ளூ	ளெ	ளே	ளை	ளொ	ளோ	ளௌ
ṟ	ற	றா	றி	றீ	று	றூ	றெ	றே	றை	றொ	றோ	றௌ
n	ன	னா	னி	னீ	னு	னூ	னெ	னே	னை	னொ	னோ	னௌ

ADDITIONAL LETTERS AND CONTRACTIONS.

ஷ்	ஷ	ஷி	ஷீ	ஸ்	ஸ	ஃ	மீ	வரு	உ
sh	shâ	shĭ	shî	s	să	ch	Month	Year	Om ᵃ sacred word

NUMERALS.

க	உ	ரு	ச	ரு	சா	எ	அ	கூ	ம	ற	௹
1	2	3	4	5	6	7	8	9	10	100	1000

Examples of compound numbers, ௰க = 11, ௰உ = 12 etc.

ZEND

BURMESE

FORM	SOUND	FORM	SOUND
ᴀ	a	ς	z
ᴀᴡ	à	ⱬ	ñ
ᴊ	i	∾	t
ⱦ	î	ⱨ	ṭ
⸃	u	ⱱ	th
ⱳ	ù	ᴗ	d
⸔	e (e)	ⱬ	dh
ⱬ	è	ⱀ	u
ᴡ	è	ⱬ	p
ⱡ	o	ⱬ	f
ⱦ	ò	ⱬ	b
ᴊᴡ	ào	ⱬ	m
ⱬ	aṅ	ⱱ	y initial
ⱬ	k	ⱬ	y medial
ᴅ	kh	ⱱ	r
ⱬ	q	ⱬ	v initial
ⱬ	g	ⱱ	v medial
ⱬ	gh	ⱬ	w
ⱬ	ṅ	ⱬ	ç
ⱬ	c (ch)	ⱬ	sh
ⱬ	j	ⱬ	s
ⱬ	sh	ⱬ	h

PUNCTUATION.

°

VOWELS

FORM	SOUND	FORM	SOUND
အ	a	(ာ	è
အာ	à	အဲ	ey
ဣ	ie	ေဩာ	äü
ဤ	ee	ေဪ	au
ဥ	u o	ဩ	äṇ
ဦ	ù ōō	အား	àḷ

CONSONANTS

FORM	SOUND	FORM	SOUND
က	k	ဒ	d
ခ	kh	ဓ	dh
ဂ	g	န	n
ဃ	gh	ပ	p
င	ng & gn	ဖ	ph
စ	ch	ဗ	b
ဆ	chh	ဘ	bh
ဇ	j	မ	m
ဈ	jh	ယ	y
ဉ	ñ	ရ	r
ဋ	ṭ	လ	l
ဌ	ṭh	ဝ	w
ဍ	ḍ	သ	s
ဎ	ḍh	ဟ	h
ဏ	ṇ	ဠ	ḷ
တ	t	အံ	aṇ
ထ	th		

CANARESE (CARNÀTACA).

This language, belonging to the Dràvidian family, is spoken throughout the plateau of Mysore, in some of the western districts of the Nizam territory, and in the district of Canara on the Malabar coast.

ಅ	a	ಏ	ê	ಙ	nga	ತ	ta	ಯ	ya
ಆ	â	ಐ	ai	ಚ	cha	ಥ	tha	ರ	ra
ಇ	i (ee)	ಒ	o	ಛ	chha	ದ	da	ಲ	la
ಈ	í (êë)	ಓ	ô	ಜ	ja	ಧ	dha	ವ	va
ಉ	u (oo)	ಔ	au	ಝ	jha	ನ	na	ಸ	sa
ಊ	û (ôö)	ಂ	n	ಞ	ña	ಪ	pa	ಶ	sha
ಋ	r̊	ಃ	h	ಟ	t'a	ಫ	pha	ಜ	za
ೠ	r'	ಕ	ka	ಠ	t'ha	ಬ	ba	ಹ	ha
ಌ	l	ಖ	kha	ಡ	d'a	ಭ	bha	ಳ	la
ೡ	l'	ಗ	ga	ಢ	d'ha	ಮ	ma	ಷ	sha
ಎ	e	ಘ	gha	ಣ	n'a				

LIGATURES

ಕಿ	ki	ಞು	ñu	ದಾ	dà	ನ್ನ	nna	ವಾ	và
ಕು	ku	ದೆ	d'e	ದಿ	di	ಪು	pu	ವು	vu
ಕೊ	kô	ದ್ಹೊ	d'o	ದೀ	dî	ಪ್ರ	pra	ವೂ	vû
ಕ್ಷ	ksha	ಟಿ	ti	ದೆ	de	ಭು	bhu	ವೀ	vî
ಗ	ga	ಟೀ	tî	ದ್ರಿ	dri	ಮ್ಮ	mma	ವೀ	vî'
ಗಿ	gi	ತು	tu	ನ	n	ರಾ	rà	ವೈ	vai
ಗು	gu	ತೆ	te	ನಾ	nâ	ರೆ	re	ವ್ವು	vvu
ಗೆ	ge	ತೈ	tai	ನಿ	ni	ಲಾ	là	ಶಾ	shà
ಗೆ	gê	ಟ್ಟು	ttu	ನೀ	nî	ಲೂ	lû	ಷ್ಟ	sht'a
ಗೈ	gai	ತ್ತೆ	tte	ನು	nu	ಲೊ	lò	ಹೊ	hò
ಞ್	ñà	ತ್ರ	tra	ನೆ	ne	ವ	va		

GUJERATI or GUZERATTEE.

This Alphabet is derived from the Sanscrit (Devanagari) characters, from which it principally differs in the omission of the connecting lines. Gujerati is spoken in the province of Gujerat (Guzerat), especially by the Parsee inhabitants, and is considered to be the mercantile language of Western India. In modern times various Gujerati publications have appeared in Bombay.

	â		o		cha		ta		bha
					chha		tha		
	i (ee)				ja		da		ma
	u (oo)		ow		jha		dha		va
	r̥		ka		t'a		na		la
	e (ai)		kha		d'a		pa		ra
			ga		d'ha		pha		sa
			gha		n'a		ba		ça
									ha

LIGATURES

ki		ji		n'i		nû		vu	
ku		ju		n'u		pi		vû	
kû		jû		n'û		pu		li	
khi		jhi		ti		pû		lu	
khu		jhu		tu		phi		lû	
khû		jhû		tû		phu		ri	
gi		t'i		thi		phû		ru	
gu		t'u		thu		bi		rû	
gû		t'û		thû		bu		si	
ghi		t'hi		di		bû		su	
ghu		t'hu		du		bhi		sû	
ghû		t'hû		dû		bhu		çi	
chi		d'i		dhi		bhû		çu	
chu		d'u		dhu		mi		çû	
chû		d'û		dhû		mu		hi	
chhi		d'hi		ni		mû		hu	
chhu		d'hu		nu		vi		hû	
chhû		d'hû							

TELUGU

one of the branches of the Dravidian stock, is spoken along the eastern coast of India from the neighbourhood of Pulicat to Chicacole. Inland it extends to the eastern boundary of the Maratha Country and Mysore, including within its range the ceded districts and Kurnool, the greater part of the
territories of the Nizam, the Hyderabad Country and a portion of the Nagpore Country. This language
is spoken by about 14 millions.

అ a	ఒ ô	ఞ nga	త ta	ర ra
ఆ â	ఒ ĕ	చ cha	థ tha	ల la
ఇ i (ee)	ఒ o	ఛ chha	ద da	వ va
ఈ î (ĕĕ)	ఓ ô	జ ja	ధ dha	శ sa
ఉ u (oo)	ఔ no	ఝ jha	న na (soft)	ష sha
ఊ û (ôô)	ం ṅ	ఞ nya	ప pa	స sa
ఋ r̥	ః h	ట t'a	ఫ pha	హ ha
ౠ r̥̄	క ka	ఠ t'ha	బ ba	క్ష ṭa
ఌ i	ఖ kha	డ d'a	భ bha	
ౡ i'	గ ga	ఢ d'ha	మ ma	ఱ sha
ఎ e	ఘ gha	ణ n'a (hard)	య ya	? Pause

LIGATURES

కా kâ	ఝా jhâ	మా mâ	తి ti	ల, li
కు ku	ఝీ jhî	మి mi	తీ tî	లు lu
కూ kû	ఝూ jhû	ము mu	తు tu	లో lo
కో ko	ఞా ñâ	మె me	తె te	ల్ల lla
క్ష ksha	ఞు nu	మో mo	త్తు ttu	ల్లి lli
గె ge	నా nâ	మ్ము mmu	త్ర tra	వా vâ
గో gô	ని ni	యా yâ	దా dâ	వు vu
గౌ gau	నీ nî	యి yi	దీ dî	వె ve
ఘా ghâ	ను nu	యె ye	దు du	వ్వ vva
ఘు ghu	నె ne	యో yo	దె de	వ్వు vvu
ఘూ ghû	న్న nna	రా râ	దో do	సి si
ఙా ngâ	పో po	రి ri	డ్డ ddu	షా shâ
ఙు ngu	ప్పు ppu	ఞూ ñû	డ్ఢా ddhâ	ష్ట sht'a
చి chi	బా bâ	త్ఛ t'c	ధా dhâ	సా sâ
చు chu	బు bu	ద్ఉ d'u	రీ rî	స్సా ssâ
చె che	భూ bhû	ద్హు d'hu	రు ru	

BENGALI.

This Alphabet is based on the Devanagari character. In some instances the circular shape has been altered into an angular form, in others the form has been entirely changed. The Bengali language is less mixed than the neighbouring idioms.

VOWELS.		CONSONANTS.				THE VOWELS sounded after the consonants take their position before, after above and below their letters. They receive in such cases the following forms.
অ a	৯ lri	ক ka	ঙ ña	ধ dha	ল la	ꠟ á follows its cons.
আ á	৯ lrí	খ kha	ট ta	ন na	ব va	ि i precedes » »
ই i	এ e	গ ga	ঠ tha	প pa	শ sha	ী í follows » »
ঈ í	ঐ ai	ঘ gha	ড da	ফ pha	ষ sha	ু u is subjoined
উ u	ও o	ঙ nga	ঢ dha	ব ba	স sa	ূ ú » »
ঊ ú	ঔ au	চ tsha	ণ na	ভ bha	হ ha	ৃ ri » »
ঋ ri	অং aug	ছ tshha	ত ta	ম ma	ক্ষ khya	ৄ rí » »
ৠ rí	অঃ ah	জ ja	থ tha	য ya		ে e precedes »
		ঝ jha	দ da	র ra		ৈ ai »

OBSERVATIONS.

The vowel-sound of the short a is inherent in all consonants.

(birám) subjoined to a consonant causes the a to drop. A consonant moreover loses its a by being attached to the following consonant.

denotes y affixed to a consonant.

denotes r. It is placed at the top of the letter, and sounded before it.

r stands under a consonant and is pronounced after it.

over a consonant, represents its nasal sound.

denotes the word Ganesh.

denotes the name of God.

serves as a stop at the end of a sentence.

ো o take the cons. in the middle.
ৌ au take the cons. in the middle.
ং ang follows the cons.
ঃ ah follows the cons.

BÚGÍS

is supposed to be the most ancient of the languages spoken in the island of Celebes. The same Alphabet is used in the Macassar language.

a	ba	ra	la
ka	ma	cha	wa
kha	pha	ja	sa
ga	ta	a	ha
nga	da	chha	ya
pa	na	ra	

Every consonant has an inherent vowel, with which it forms a separate syllable.

The following vowels vary in position:

e before a letter.
i over a letter.
o after a letter.
u under a letter.
ung at the top of a letter.

JAVANESE

ORDINARY LETTERS			INITIAL LETTERS		
Ordin. Form	Pasangans	Sound	Ordin. Form	Pasangans	Sound
		hå		—	Nå
		nå	—		Tyå
		tyå		—	Kå
		rå			Tå
		kå	or	—	Så
		då			På
		tå		—	Nyå
		så		—	Gå
		wå		—	Bå
		lå			
		på			
		då			
		dyå			
		yå			
		nyå			
		må			
		gå			
		bå			
		tå			
		ngå			
		På-tycre', rĕ			
	---	Ngå-letet, lĕ			

UNCONNECTED VOWELS.

a   i   u   e   o

ADDITIONAL CONSONANTS.

The following four letters, with the sign ᴧ *(Sastrosworo)* at the top, occur in words derived from the Arabic, as there are no consonants in the Javanese Alphabet, which fully express these sounds.

chå   stands for the Arabic   chå

få   „ „ „ „   fe

zå   „ „ „ „   ze

ghå   „ „ „ „   ghain

NUMERALS.

1	2	3	4	5	6	7	8	9	0

VOWELS AND DIACRITICAL SIGNS,

called *Sandangan*.

Form	Name	Sound and power
⌒	Pĕpĕt	ĕ
◠	Ulu or Wulu	i
◞	Suku	u
᧗	Taling	e
᧗—꦳	Taling-Tarung	o
◡	Paten or Pánkon	(deprives a consonant of its vowel)
⟨	Ságnyan or Wignyan	h (at the end of a syllable)
⠿	Tyĕty'a	ng (at the end of a syllable)
╱	Layar	r (at the end of a syllable)
(or ⌣	Tyâkrâ	r (between a consonant and a succeeding letter)
ꦿ	Kĕrĕt	rĕ (after a consonant)
⫝̸	Pĭnkal	y (after a consonant)

PODOS or PADAS.

Under this designation the Javanese writing contains the following signs:

 Podo luhur. With this sign superiors begin their letters to inferiors.

 Podo madyo is used at the commencement of letters by persons of equal rank.

 Podo andap, with this superscription an inferior addresses a superior.

Podo-bab stands at the beginning of a new paragraph.

Podo-lingso, the usual stop at the end of a sentence or a detached word. In poetry it marks the end of verses, which are written consecutively like prose. It is doubled at the end of a section.

Podo andegging lyelatu or *dirgo mururas* occasionally replaces the *Podo-lingso*; mostly it accompanies numerals, and isolates them from the adjoining words.

Ulu munta. When the vowel of a final syllable is an *ulu,* this character takes a *Tyety'a* in the centre.

Suku mendut. When the vowel of the last syllable is a *Suku* it takes this form.

Dirgo mure is the name of the sign placed over the *Taling* or *Talīng-Tarung,* when this vowel occurs in the final syllable.

Podo wotyan anglegenno. Under this name the *Tarung* is employed as a sign of separation.

Piselep ingstembarg gede, serves to divide poetry.

 *Purwo-podo* stands at the beginning of poems.

 *Madyo-podo,* at the beginning of a song following another, when the melody and the measure are changed.

 *Wasono-podo* at the end of a poem.

LIGATURES.

The following ligatures consist of the (Vowel-) signs *Suku*, *Tyokro*, *Keret* and *Pinkal* combined with the ordinary characters and *Pansangans*. The diacritical marks are also added.

○   The small pasangan *Wo* is placed below a letter standing in the third row.

ʃ 、 ﹂   These small diacritical marks are placed under auxiliary letters which stand in the third row.

∕   The short *Layar* is employed when there is no room for the large *Layar*.

∠   This mark is placed under the letters *Wo* and *Ngo* to form the vowels *u* and *o*.

OBSERVATIONS.

The Javanese language has 20 letters which are called *Aksoro*, *Sastro* or *Tjarakan*. They are written from left to right, without being joined together. By the many auxiliary letters, vowels and diacritical signs, the numbers of characters is considerably increased. The *Pasangans*, employed in the Alphabet, are in close connexion with the sign *Paten*, which in fact they replace. When a consonant occurs in the middle of a word, and is to be deprived of its vowel, a *Paten* must be employed. To obviate a disjunction arising from the use of this sign, the *Paten* is omitted, but the letter, which follows the mute consonant, is changed in form or in position or in both. The substituting sign is then called *Pasangan*. The *Pasangans* being mostly placed under the common letters, while some vowels and diacritical signs figure above the letters, the Javanese writing runs within three rows. The position of a character in one row or an other is indicated in this Alphabet by the addition of dots.

TIBETAN

Form	Value	Form	Value
ཀ	k	མ	m
ཁ	kh	ཙ	ts
ག	g	ཚ	tsh
ང	ng	ཛ	s
ཆ	ch	ཝ	w
ཆྷ	chh	ཞ	j (French)
ཇ	j	ཟ	z
ཉ	nya	འ	ha
ཏ	t	ཡ	y
ཐ	th	ར	r
ད	d	ལ	l
ན	n	ཤ	sh
པ	p	ས	s
ཕ	ph	ཧ	h
བ	b	ཨ	a

VOWELS.

The Tibetan language is read from left to right and has five vowels. The vowel **a** is inherent in the several consonants. When confusion is apprehended from the absence of a distinct **a** after the prefixes

ག ད བ མ

the sign འ is inserted to denote **a**. The remaining vowels are written and named as follows,

ི gigu i
ུ zhabs-kyu u
ེ drengbu e
ོ naro o

The *gigu drengbu* and *naro* are placed above their consonants, the *zhabs-kyu* below them. When double, the *zhabs-kyu* is pronounced **uu** or **ow**; double *drengbu* **ay** or **ie**; double *naro* **oo** or **ou**. *Gigu* is often formed thus ྀ

ྭ is placed below the letters. **Ph** is changed by it into **f**; **ss** into **x**. Under the other letters it represents the vowel **a**; according to others it denotes **u**.

ོ placed over **th**, **a** and **h** denotes with the first of these letters **mce** with the other two **m**. According to others it signifies **ang** and **ong**.

ACCENTS.

ྼ guttural sign
ྻ palatal »
ྃ nasal »
྾ sign of the singular number.

PUNCTUATION.

༄༅ is an introductory sign. Besides this figure other varieties are in use.

། Comma. Two such signs are equal to a full stop. Four such strokes, with ༈ between them, denote "the end".

྾ is inserted between the syllables.

༼ ༽ mark the stress of a word.

LIGATURES.

 སྒྱ སྒ སྒྲ སྒྱ སྐྱ སྒྱ སྐྱ སྒྱ སྒྱ སྒྱ སྒྱ སྐྱ སྒ སྒྱ

7

MANTSIIU

Name	Value
Sha	sh
Ta	t
Da	d
Te	t
De	d
La	l
Ma	m
Cha	ch
Ja	j
Ya	y
Ke	k
Ge	g
Khe	kh guttural
Ra	r

Form: uncombined, initial, medial, final

Name	Value
A	a
E	e
I	i
O	o
U	u
O	ö
An	an
Na	n
Ka	k
Ga	g aspirated
Kha	kh guttural
Ba	b soft
Pa	p aspirated
Za	z

(A, E, I, O, U, O: as in German)

Form: uncombined, initial, medial, final

MANTSHU

LIGATURES

unconnected	initial	medial	final	Value
				bi
				bo
				bu
				bo long
				pi
				po
				pu
				po long
				ki
				ku
				me
	i	ma	mu iml	re
gge	mi iail	mi	ml	rl
gk	mo	mo	al	ye

Name	unconnected	initial	medial	final	Value
Fa				:	f
Wa				:	w
Dze				:	dz
Tze				:	tz
Zha				:	j (French)
Se				:	s
Chha				:	chh
Jha				:	jh

CONSONANTS BEFORE CONSONANTS.

n	k	t

DIPHTHONGS.

	na
	ne
ui	
oa	
oi	
öi	
ai	
ci	

ACCENTS.

softens the sound.

changes the letters into gutturals.

PUNCTUATION.

, equal to semicolon.

" equal to full stop.

THE NUMERALS

are composed of letters, as

1   10   100

TheMantshu characters are written from the top downwards. The lines are read from left to right, as

a   sere   khergen

MONGOLIAN

CONSONANTS				VOWELS			
Initial	Medial	Final	Value	Initial	Medial	Final	Value
ꭍ	ꭍ	ꭍ	n	᠊	᠊	᠊ 7	a
᠊	᠊	᠊	b	᠊	᠊	᠊ 7	e
᠊	᠊	. . . .	ch Scotch	᠊	᠊	᠊	i
᠊	᠊	. . . .	gh guttural	᠊	᠊	᠊	o
ꭍ	ꭍ	᠊	k	᠊	᠊	᠊	u
ꭍ	ꭍ	. . . .	g	᠊	᠊	᠊	ö
᠊	᠊	᠊	m	᠊	᠊	᠊	ü
᠊	᠊	᠊	l				
᠊	᠊	᠊	r				
᠊	᠊	᠊	t				
᠊	᠊	᠊	d				
᠊	᠊	. . . .	y				
᠊	᠊	. . . .	z, dz				
᠊	᠊	. . . .	ts or ch				
᠊	᠊	᠊	s				
᠊	᠊	. . . .	sh				
᠊	᠊	. . . .	w				

(right brace after the vowel values:) as in German.

PUNCTUATION.

᠊᠊ This sign divides sentences.

∴ is used at the end of a period.

Mongolian books are not numbered by the page but by the folio. It is usual to head each folio by ꭍ or some other mark like this.

OBSERVATIONS.

Like the Mantshu the Mongolian characters are written in perpendicular lines from left to right. The Alphabet consists of seven vowels, together with diphthongs derived from them, and of seventeen consonants which vary in form according to their position at the beginning, the middle, and the end of a word; or according to the effect exercised upon them by certain orthographical rules. — The consonants are not regarded as isolated sounds, but are always joined to vowels with which they form simple syllables. An exception is made to this rule when a consonant occurs as the final of a syllable or a word. But even such final consonants may be attended by a vowel. A variation of the Mongolian characters is known under the name of *Galik*.

ARMENIAN

Form		Name	Value	Num.-power	Form		Name	Value	Num.-power
Ա	ա	Jpe	a	1	Մ	մ	mien	m	200
Բ	բ	pien	p	2	Յ	յ	he or ye	h or y (in toy)	300
Գ	գ	kim	k ck	3	Ն	ն	noo	n	400
Դ	դ	tah	t (soft)	4	Շ	շ	shah	sh	500
Ե	ե	yetch	y (cons.)	5	Ո	ո	wo	WO (in word) or O (in move)	600
Զ	զ	zah	z	6	Չ	չ	tchah	tch	700
Է	է	è	e (in met)	7	Պ	պ	bé	b	800
Ը	ը	yet	e (in paper)	8	Ջ	ջ	tché	ch (soft)	900
Թ	թ	twoh	t (hard)	9	Ռ	ռ	rah	r (hard)	1000
Ժ	ժ	zhe	j (French)	10	Ս	ս	sé	s	2000
Ի	ի	inni	i (in ill)	20	Վ	վ	viev	v	3000
Լ	լ	lune	l	30	Տ	տ	dune	d	4000
Խ	խ	khe	ch (German)	40	Ր	ր	ré	r (soft)	5000
Ծ	ծ	dzah	z (Italian)	50	Ց	ց	tzvoh	tz (hard)	6000
Կ	կ	ghien	g (hard)	60	Ւ	ւ	une	u (in due)	7000
Հ	հ	kwoh	h	70	Փ	փ	pure	p	8000
Ձ	ձ	tzah	tz (soft)	80	Ք	ք	ké	k	9000
Ղ	ղ	ghahd	γ (Romaic)	90	Օ	օ	o	o	10000
Ճ	ճ	jé	j	100	Ֆ	ֆ	pha	f	20000

LIGATURES.

ﬓ hn	ﬔ ls	ﬕ me	ﬖ mi	ﬗ mn
Լ yev	﬘ lu	﬙ mg	﬚ mye	﬛ vn

ACCENTS and PUNCTUATIONS.

´ acute	' apostrophe	‿ sign of length
` grave	, comma	° sign of brevity and abbreviation
ˆ circumflex	։ colon or semicolon	
˘ rough breathing	․ full stop	̔ sign of abbreviation, it also converts a letter into a numeral.
̓ soft breathing	֊ hyphen	

GEORGIAN.

The Georgian language is written in two Alphabets. The ancient character, used in the Bible and ecclesiastical works, is called *Khūtsūri* (i. e. sacerdotal). The character *Mkhedrūli* (or rather *Mkhedrūli khéli i. e.* Soldier's hand) is used in ordinary writing and printing.

KHŪTSŪRI				MKHEDRŪLI					
Form	Value	Form	Value	Form	Name	Value	Form	Name	Value
Ⴀ ⴀ	a	Ⴑ ⴑ	s	ა	an	a	უ	un	oo
Ⴁ ⴁ	b	Ⴒ ⴒ	t	ბ	ban	b	უ̂		w
Ⴂ ⴂ	g	ႭჃ ⴍⴣ	oo	გ	gan	g	ჳ	vĕ	vĕ
Ⴃ ⴃ	d	Ⴣ ⴣ	v	დ	don	d	ფ	phar	ph
Ⴄ ⴄ	e	Ⴔ ⴔ	p'h	ე	en	e	ქ	khan	kh
Ⴅ ⴅ	w	Ⴕ ⴕ	k	ვ	win	v	ღ	ghan	gh (غ Arab.)
Ⴆ ⴆ	z	Ⴖ ⴖ	gh (Arab.)	ზ	zen	z	ყ	qar	q (ق Arab.)
Ⴡ ⴡ	h, ĕ (short)	Ⴗ ⴗ	q	ჱ	he	e	შ	shin	sh
Ⴇ ⴇ	th	Ⴘ ⴘ	sh	თ	than	th	ჩ	chin	ch
Ⴈ ⴈ	i	Ⴙ ⴙ	ch	ი	in	i	ც	tzan	tz
Ⴉ ⴉ	k'	Ⴚ ⴚ	ts	კ	kan	k	ძ	dzil	dz
Ⴊ ⴊ	l	Ⴛ ⴛ	ds	ლ	las	l	წ	thzil	thz
Ⴋ ⴋ	m	Ⴜ ⴜ	thz	მ	man	m	ჭ	jar	j
Ⴌ ⴌ	n	Ⴞ ⴞ	kh	ნ	nar	n	ხ	khan	kh (rough)
Ⴢ ⴢ	i (short)	Ⴤ ⴤ	khh	ჲ	ie	i (short)	ჴ	khhar	khh (very rough)
Ⴍ ⴍ	o	Ⴟ ⴟ	j	ო	on	o	ჯ	jan	j
Ⴎ ⴎ	p	[illegible]	h (mute)	პ	par	p	ჰ	hae	h
Ⴏ ⴏ	j (French)	Ⴥ ⴥ	ho	ჟ	zhan	j (French)	ჵ	hoe	hoi
Ⴐ ⴐ	r	Ⴝ ⴝ	ch	რ	rae	r	ჶ	fa	f
				ს	san	s	ჷ	short e	
				ტ	tar	t			

PUNCTUATION.

- Hyphen	։ Full stop
։· End of a Period	. Semicolon

, Comma.

GREEK

Form	Name	Value	Accents and Punctuation
A α	Alpha	a	
B β	Beta	b	
Γ γ	Gamma	g	
Δ δ	Delta	d	
E ε	Epsilon	e short	
Z ζ	Zeta	z	
H η	Eta	e long	
Θ ϑ θ	Theta	th	
I ι	Iota	i	
K κ	Kappa	k	
Λ λ	Lambda	l	
M μ	My	m	
N ν	Ny	n	
Ξ ξ	Xi	x	
O ο	Omikron	o short	
Π π	Pi	p	
P ρ	Rho	r	
Σ σ ς	Sigma	s	
T τ	Tau	t	
Y υ	Ypsilon	u	
Φ φ	Phi	f ph	
X χ	Chi	ch	
Ψ ψ	Psi	ps	
Ω ω	Omega	o long	

SPIRITS OR BREATHINGS.

Every Greek word, commencing with a vowel, has over this initial either

(') spiritus lenis, the soft breathing,

or (‛) spiritus asper, the rough breathing.

The former is aspirated before a vowel and equal to our h. The spiritus lenis is placed over an unaspirated initial vowel. When a word commences with a diphthong (αι, ει, οι, υι, αυ, ευ, ην, ου, ωυ), the breathings as well as the accents are placed over the second vowel, as αὗτος, οἷος, εἰκών. ρ always has the rough breathing at the beginning of a word. In the middle of a word, when this letter is doubled, the first ρ has the soft and the second the rough breathing, as ῤῥ.

ACCENTS.

′ acute or sharp sound.

‛ grave or heavy sound.

̑ circumflex or long and trailing sound.

Accents, combined with either of the breathings or with the diaeresis, are marked in the following manner,

PUNCTUATION AND OTHER MARKS.

The point and comma are used in Greek as in English. There is no semicolon. The Colon is denoted by a dot over the line (˙). The note of interrogation is (;). In some modern editons the note of exclamation (!) has been introduced.

The Comma is also used to distinguish two words of equal spelling. As ὅ,τι, τό,τε, differing form the particles ὅτι, τοτε. This sign is termed Diastole or Hyper-diastole.

The following signs are used in connexion with letters and syllables. The Apostrophe ('), the Diæresis (¨), over a vowel separated from the sound of a preceding vowel, and the Coronis ' in contracted words to denote a Crasis as τοὐναντίον for τὸ ἐναντίον.

Iota subscriptum is the Iota under the vowels ᾳ, ῃ, ῳ, and indicates the etymology of the words. Formerly this ι was pronounced, and had its place by the side of the vowel. This lateral Iota is still used in words spelled with capital letters, as THI ΣΟΦΙΑ (for τῇ σοφιᾳ) ῌΑιδης (ᾅδης).

NUMERALS.

The Greeks employed the letters of the alphabet to denote the numerals, but as these characters were not sufficient for this purpose, the ϛ (Βαῦ, Vau) or Ϝ (Digamma) was inserted after the ε, the Ϟ (Κόππα) after π, and Ϡ (Σαμπῖ) after ω. The letters employed as numerals are distinguished by a top line sloping, to the right as α´ 1, β´ 2, ϛ´ 6, ι´ 10, ια´ 11, κ´ 20, κϛ´ 26, ρ´ 100, σ´ 200, σλβ´ 232 etc. The thousands recommence with α, and have a stroke below on the left, as ͵α 1000, ͵βσλβ´ 2232.

OBSERVATIONS.

γ before γ and the other palatals (κ χ ξ) is pronounced like n, as ἐγγύς (eng-gus).

ι is a mere vowel and never represents the consonantal sound of y, as Ἰωνία (I-onia). In foreign words the deficient consonant was replaced by ι, as Ἰούλιος (Julius).

σ is an initial and medial s. The final is marked by the sign of ς. The latter is, in some modern editions, used at the end of medial syllables.

τ before ι, followed by a vowel, retains its proper sound of ti, and is not pronounced like shi, as Γαλατια (Ga-la-ti-a).

GREEK LIGATURES AND ABBREVIATIONS.

These contractions are peculiar to old editions of Greek works. They are no longer used in modern typography.

⟨lig⟩	αι	⟨lig⟩	εἶναι	⟨lig⟩	ου	⟨lig⟩	οτι
⟨lig⟩	αν	⟨lig⟩	ἐκ	⟨lig⟩	οὐδε	⟨lig⟩	οτο
⟨lig⟩	αλ	⟨lig⟩	ελ	⟨lig⟩	οὐκ	⟨lig⟩	οτρ
⟨lig⟩	αλλ	⟨lig⟩	ελλ	⟨lig⟩	οὐτοῦ	⟨lig⟩	οτυ
⟨lig⟩	ἄν	⟨lig⟩	ἔλαττον	⟨lig⟩	π	⟨lig⟩	οτω
⟨lig⟩	ἀπο	⟨lig⟩	ἐν	⟨lig⟩	παρὰ	⟨lig⟩	συ
⟨lig⟩	ἀρ	⟨lig⟩	ἐξ	⟨lig⟩	πει	⟨lig⟩	σω
⟨lig⟩	ας	⟨lig⟩	ἐπειδὴ	⟨lig⟩	περ	⟨lig⟩	τ
⟨lig⟩	αὐ	⟨lig⟩	ἐπευ	⟨lig⟩	περὶ	⟨lig⟩	τα
⟨lig⟩	αὐτοῦ	⟨lig⟩	ἐπὶ	⟨lig⟩	πην	⟨lig⟩	ται
⟨lig⟩	αὐτῷ	⟨lig⟩	ἐπι	⟨lig⟩	ππ	⟨lig⟩	ταῖς
⟨lig⟩	β	⟨lig⟩	ἐστι	⟨lig⟩	πρ	⟨lig⟩	ταῦτα
⟨lig⟩	γ	⟨lig⟩	ευ	⟨lig⟩	προ	⟨lig⟩	τει
⟨lig⟩	γα	⟨lig⟩	ην	⟨lig⟩	πτ	⟨lig⟩	την
⟨lig⟩	γὰρ	⟨lig⟩	ϑ	⟨lig⟩	πυ	⟨lig⟩	τὴν
⟨lig⟩	γγ	⟨lig⟩	ϑα	⟨lig⟩	πω	⟨lig⟩	τῆς
⟨lig⟩	γγ	⟨lig⟩	ϑε	⟨lig⟩	ρα	⟨lig⟩	τι
⟨lig⟩	γε	⟨lig⟩	ϑει	⟨lig⟩	ρι	⟨lig⟩	το
⟨lig⟩	γει	⟨lig⟩	ϑη	⟨lig⟩	ρο	⟨lig⟩	το
⟨lig⟩	γελ	⟨lig⟩	ϑι	⟨lig⟩	σ	⟨lig⟩	τὸ
⟨lig⟩	γελλ	⟨lig⟩	ϑο	⟨lig⟩	σα	⟨lig⟩	τὸν
⟨lig⟩	γεν	⟨lig⟩	ϑυ	⟨lig⟩	σαῦτα	⟨lig⟩	του
⟨lig⟩	γερ	⟨lig⟩	ϑω	⟨lig⟩	σε	⟨lig⟩	τοῦ
⟨lig⟩	γη	⟨lig⟩	καὶ	⟨lig⟩	σει	⟨lig⟩	τοῦ
⟨lig⟩	γι	⟨lig⟩	καὶ	⟨lig⟩	ση	⟨lig⟩	τοῦ
⟨lig⟩	γίνεται	⟨lig⟩	καὶ	⟨lig⟩	σην	⟨lig⟩	τρο
⟨lig⟩	γν	⟨lig⟩	κατὰ	⟨lig⟩	σϑ	⟨lig⟩	ττ
⟨lig⟩	γο	⟨lig⟩	κατὰ	⟨lig⟩	σϑαι	⟨lig⟩	τυ
⟨lig⟩	γρ	⟨lig⟩	κεφάλαιον	⟨lig⟩	σχ	⟨lig⟩	τῳ
⟨lig⟩	γυ	⟨lig⟩	λλ	⟨lig⟩	σι	⟨lig⟩	τῷ
⟨lig⟩	γω	⟨lig⟩	μάτων	⟨lig⟩	σκ	⟨lig⟩	τῶν
⟨lig⟩	δ	⟨lig⟩	μὲν	⟨lig⟩	σο	⟨lig⟩	τῶν
⟨lig⟩	δὲ	⟨lig⟩	μὲν	⟨lig⟩	σο	⟨lig⟩	ῦ
⟨lig⟩	δευ	⟨lig⟩	μένος	⟨lig⟩	σπ	⟨lig⟩	υι
⟨lig⟩	δεξ	⟨lig⟩	μετὰ	⟨lig⟩	σπαν	⟨lig⟩	υν
⟨lig⟩	δια	⟨lig⟩	μετὰ	⟨lig⟩	σσ	⟨lig⟩	ὑπ
⟨lig⟩	διὰ	⟨lig⟩	μῶν	⟨lig⟩	στ	⟨lig⟩	ὑπο
⟨lig⟩	δρ	⟨lig⟩	οἶον	⟨lig⟩	στα	⟨lig⟩	χαν
⟨lig⟩	ει	⟨lig⟩	ος	⟨lig⟩	στε	⟨lig⟩	χι
⟨lig⟩	ει			⟨lig⟩	στει	⟨lig⟩	χρ
				⟨lig⟩	στη	⟨lig⟩	ψι

ROMAIC or MODERN GREEK.

The Alphabet consists of the following 24 letters, which are the same as in ancient Greek.

Α α, Β β, Γ γ, Δ δ, Ε ε, Ζ ζ, Η η, Θ ϑ, Ι ι, Κ κ, Λ λ, Μ μ, Ν ν, Ξ ξ,
Ο ο, Π π, Ρ ρ, Σ σ (final ς), Τ τ, Υ υ, Φ φ, Χ χ, Ψ ψ, Ω ω.

The vowels are α, ε, η, ι, ο, υ and ω.

PRONUNCIATION.

Α α *(Alpha)* short or long as in *papa*.

Β β *(Vita)* is represented by *bh* or *v*. In sound it differs slightly from the English *v*, the mouth being somewhat rounded in the articulation of the Romaic letter.

Γ γ *(Gamma)* is an aspirate of *g* in *go*. In γγ the first gamma becomes nasal; αγγελος, for instance, is pronounced *ang-ye-los*. It receives the same sound before the palatals κ ξ and χ, as αναγκη *(a-nang-ki)*. Before ε ι and υ it is like *y* in *yes*. To produce the sound of our *g* in *grey*, the Modern Greeks use Γκ as Γκράϊχμ *(Graham)*.

Δ δ *(Delta)* is aspirated as *th* in the.

Ε ε *(Epsilon)* as the *e* in *pet*.

Ζ ζ *(Zita)* like *z*. Ζωή *(zo-i)*.

Θ ϑ *(Thita)* like *th* in *thick*.

Ι ι *(Iota)* like *i* in *machine*. When ι is placed under the vowels as in η υ ω or by the side of capital vowels (Αι, Ηι, Ωι) it is not sounded and only lengthens the principal vowel. This ι is known as the *Iota subscriptum*.

Κ κ *(Kappa)* like our *k*. It is softened after the nasal γ hence αγκιλά is pronounced *anglii*.

Λ λ *(Lameda)* like *l* in *long*. Before ι it has the sound of *lli* in *William*.

Μ μ *(Mi)* like *m*. Placed before π, these two letters acquire the sound of *b* μπαρούτι *(barooti)*. This combination of μπ takes the sound of *b* in words received from foreign languages, but in compound Romaic words, each letter retains its original pronunciation. Example εμπόρευμα *(em-pee-ree-ma)*.

Ν ν *(Ni)* is *n*. Placed before τ, the two letters coalesce in the sound of *d*, which is articulated somewhat harder than the *d*. For example ντιβάνι *(diwani)*. ντ have conjointly the sound of *j*; as ντζαμι *(Jami)*. When the letters ν and τ form part of two syllables in a compound word, they retain their natural sound of *nt*. For example εντιμος *(en-timos)*. Before the vowel ι the ν is articulated like *ni* in *opinion* as νίπτω *(nyipto)*.

Ξ ξ *(Xi)* is *X*.

Ο ο *(Onikron)* like *o* in *dot*.

Π π *(Pi)* like *p*.

Ρ ρ *(Ro)* like *r* in *rod*. If doubled, it has a sharper sound.

Σ σ *(Sigma)* like *s* in *so*. Before Β, Γ, Δ, Ζ, Λ, Μ, Ν, Ρ and in the proclitics (such as τούς τάς) before the same consonants, the Sigma is sounded like *z*, as Σμύρνη *(Zmirni)*.

Τ τ *(Taph)* is *t*. τζ sounds sometimes like *ts*, but generally like *ch*, as τζελεπης *(chelepis)*. Words with τζ are mostly of foreign origin.

Υ υ *(Ypsilon)* lik *y* in *Egypt*. For example τρυφλιον *(triflion)*.

Φ φ *(Phi)* like *f* or *ph*.

Χ χ *(Khi* or *Chi)* like the German or Scotch *ch*. Before the vowels α, ε, ο, ω, it is more harsh than before *e* and *i*.

Ψ ψ *(Psi)* like *ps* in *gipsy*.

Ω ω *(Omega)* like the long *o*.

The following are diphthongs αι, αυ, ει, ευ, ηυ, οι and ου *(u)*. Αι sounds like *e* in *ethics*. The υ

of αυ, ευ, ηυ sounds like β before a vowel, or the soft and liquid letters β, γ, δ, ζ, λ, μ, ν, ρ. — οι is like *ee* and ου like *oo* in *good*.

The diæresis over the second vowel of diphthongs restores to each vowel its original sound; αϊ, αϋ, τϊ, εϋ are pronounced separately α-ι, α-υ &c.

BREATHINGS AND PUNCTUATION.

The Romaic or Modern Greek admits like the ancient language two marks over initial vowels, namely the *Smooth breathing Spiritus lenis* ('), which is not noticed in reading, and the *Rough breathing Spiritus asper* ('), which in classical Greek takes the sound of our *h*, but is not audible in the modern language. The ρ, as an initial, is invariably marked with the *rough breathing*. In double ρ the first has the *smooth* and the second the *rough breathing*.

The names of the stops are, τελεια, full stop (.), μισοστιγμή colon (·), ὑποστιγμή or ὑποδιαστολή comma (,) and σημείον ἐρωτήσεως sign of interrogation (;). The mark of exclamation (!) is rarely used.

To these signs must be added the *apostrophe* and the *diæresis*. The former (') denotes the elision of one or more vowels. E. g. ἀπ' ἐμένα, ἀφ' ἡμᾶς instead of ἀπο etc. This elision of vowels occurs even before consonants as 'απ' τή instead of ἀπὸ τή.

In κἄν (instead of καὶ ἄν) and κἄντνας (instead of καὶ ἄν ἕνας) etc, the mark (') denotes the coalescence of vowels (κρᾶσις) and is called *coronix*. This mark is often used in contractions as μ̄ούκαμ-ψαν τὸ χέρι.

The diæresis prevents the union of diphthongs. E. g. μπαϊαντζήζ sounds *bo-y-an-jis*.

Another mark of separation is the *diastole* (·), which resembles the comma, and is used to distinguish the pronoun ὅ, τι and the adverb τό, τε from the conjunction ὅτι and the adverb τότε.

ACCENTS.

The tone is indicated by three accents, namely the *circumflex* (περισπωμένη) ˜ or long accent, the *acute* (ὀγεία) or sharp accent, and the *grave* (βαρεΐα) or heavy accent in final syllables. Some monosyllabic words, being unaccented, are called *atona*. The *circumflex* can only be placed on the ultimate and penultimate syllable. When the vowel of a final syllable is long, the penultimate vowel cannot take the circumflex. A word is termed *perispomenon*, when it has the circumflex on its last syllable, or if it is a monosyllable and is marked with this accent. When the circumflex occurs over the penult, the word is *properispomenon*.

The *Acute* takes its place in the penultimate and ante-penultimate syllable. Also on the final syllable at the end of a period, or when an enclitic follows (ί, ε, a word like μοῦ, μοί, μέ which throws its accent on the antecedent).

When the final syllable is long, the acute cannot revert to the ante-penultimate.

When the acute occurs in a monosyllable or in a final syllable, the word is called *oxytonon*; the penultimate, thus accented, is called *paroxytonon*; and the ante-penultimate with the acute is *proparoxytonon*.

OLD-SLAVONIC (CYRILLIC).

Based on the most ancient MSS, and cut under the direction of the I. R. Aulic Councillor
Dr. Paul Jos. Schafarik at the type-factory of Gottlieb Haase Söhne in Prague.

Form		Name	Value	Form		Name	Value
А	а	Az	a	Ф	ф	Fert	f, ph
Б	б	Buky	b	Х	х	Chĕr	kh
В	в	Vĕdi	v	Ѡ	ѡ	Ó	ó
Г	г	Glagol'	g	Ѿ	ѿ	Ot	ot
Д	д	Dobro	d	Ц	ц	Ci	ts
Є	є	Est'	e	Ч	ч	Červ'	č
Ж	ж	Živĕte	ž	Ш	ш	Ša	š
Ѕ	ѕ	Zĕlo	z	Щ	щ	Šta	št, šč
Ꙁ	ꙁ	Zemlja	z	Ъ	ъ	Jer	—
И	и	Iže	i	Ы	ы	Jery	y
Ї	ї	I	i	Ы	ы	Jery	y
I	ι	I	i, y	Ь	ь	Jerek	—
К	к	Kako	k	Ѣ	ѣ	Jeť	ĕ
Л	л	Ljudi	l	Ю	ю	Ju	yu
М	м	Myslite	m	Ꙗ	ꙗ	Ja	ya
Н	н	Naš	n	Ѥ	ѥ	Je	ye
О	о	On	o	Ѧ	ѧ	Ęs	ę
П	п	Pokoj	p	Ѫ	ѫ	Ąs	ą
Р	р	Rci (Reci)	r	Ѩ	ѩ	Jęs	yę
С	с	Slovo	s	Ѭ	ѭ	Jąs	yą
Т	т	Tverdo	t	Ѯ	ѯ	Ksi	x
Ћ	ћ	Tĕrv'	ť	Ѱ	ѱ	Psi	ps
Оу	оу	Uk	u	Ѳ	ѳ	Thita	th
Ꙋ	ꙋ	Uk	u	Ѵ	ѵ	Ižica	y

NUMERICAL LETTERS.

а· ·в· ·г· ·д· ·є· etc. ·аι· ·вι· ·гι· ·дι· ·єι· etc. ·ка· ·кв· ·кг· ·кд· ·кє· etc.
1 2 3 4 5   11 12 13 14 15   21 22 23 24 25
ѕ = ѕ = 6   ҁ = ч = 90   ҂ = 1 000, E. g. ҂ѕтчѕ = 6396.

ABBREVIATIONS (In Slavonic Titly).

·· Titla (simple).   ⌢ Glagol'-Titla.   ⌢ Oneček.
⌢ Dobro-Titla.   ⌢ Slovo-Titla.   ι Pajerek.

NOTES.

1) The power and pronunciation of the accented (Roman) characters are sufficiently explained in the Polish and Czechian Alphabets.

2) The alphabetical names have been rectified and, as regards the nasals, completed according to approved ancient authorities.

3) The characters are designed to be printed without the abbreviations, which as relics of the middle ages must be restricted to ecclesiastical works. Here they are solely introduced as historical forms. The "Pajerek" is a Jer or Jerek placed over a letter.

4) As in ancient MSS, the numbers are indicated by the insertion of the letters between two dots. The "Titla" formerly used have thus become unnecessary.

GLAGOLITIC.

According to ancient MSS (see. XI—XII) designed by Dr. Paul Jos. Schafarik, cut at the type-factory of Gottlieb Haase Söhne in Prague.

Form		Name	Value		Num: value	Form		Name	Value		Num: value
			Cyrill.	Latin					Cyrill.	Latin	
✦	✦	Az	а	a	1	Ꙋ	ꙋ	Uk	оу	u	400
Ⱇ	ⱇ	Buky	б	b	2	Ф	ф	Fert	ф	f, ph	500
Ꞁ	ⱏ	Vĕdi	в	v	3	Ⱇ	ⱇ				
℅	℅	Glagol'	г	g	4	Ⱒ	ⱒ	Chèr	х	ch	600
ⰴ	ⰴ	Dobro	д	d	5	Ⱁ	ⱁ	Ó	ω	ó	700
Э	э	Est	е	e	6	Ⱋ	ⱋ	Šta	щ	št	800
Ж	ж	Živĕte	ж	ž	7	Ⱌ	ⱌ	Ci	ц	c	900
✦	✦	Zĕlo	s	z	8	Ⱍ	ⱍ	Červ'	ч	č	1000
Ⰸ	ⰸ	Zemlja	з	z	9	Ⱎ	ⱎ	Ša	ш	š	
Ⱙ	ⱙ	lže	и	i	10						
Ꙗ	ꙗ	I	і	i	20	Ⰱ	ⰱ	Jer	ъ	o̷/ĕ	
Ⰴ	ⰴ	Dĕrv' o. / Jot	ђ, і	dj, j	30	Ꙑ	ꙑ	Jery	ы	y	
Ⱂ	ⱂ	Kako	к	k	40	Ⰹ	ⰹ	Jerek	ь	e̷/ï	
ⰴ	ⰴ	Ljudi	л	l	50	Ⰰ	ⰰ	Jet	ĕ	è, ja	
Ⱞ	ⱞ	Myslite	м	m	60	Ⱓ	ⱓ	Ju	ю	ju	
Ⱂ	ⱂ	Naš	н	n	70	Є	є	Es	ѧ	ę	
Ⱛ	ⱛ	On	о	o	80	Ⰾ	ⰾ	As	ѫ	ą	
Ⱂ	ⱂ	Pokoj	п	p	90	Ⰿ	ⰿ	Jes	ѩ	ję	
Ⰱ	ⰱ	R'ci	р	r	100	Ⱖ	ⱖ	Jąs	ѭ	ją	
Ⱊ	ⱊ	Slovo	с	s	200	Ⱚ	ⱚ	Thita	ѳ	th	
Ⱓ	ⱓ	Tvr'do	т	t	300	Ⱛ	ⱛ	Ižica	ѵ	y	

NOTES.

1. The letter *Jery* is a compound of *Jer* and *Iže*.
2. The letters Ⱎ—ⰿ and ⰵ—ⰹ are duplicate forms. Ⱎ and ⰵ are peculiar to Bulgarian MSS; ⰿ and ⰹ are Croatian characters. ⰴ on the other hand is not a real duplicate form of ф, it being identical with ✦, which is used *instead* of ф.
3. These characters are arranged to be printed without abbreviations, which are confined to liturgical books.
4. The numerical power of the letters is indicated by dots on both sides, as ·✦· ·Ⱇ· etc.
5. Further information on the value and the pronunciation of the accented letters is given in the Czechian and Polish Alphabets.

CROATO-GLAGOLITIC.

Designed from Croatian MSS and printed works by Dr. PAUL JOS. SCHAFARIK; cut at the type-factory of GOTTLIEB HAASE SÖHNE in Prague.

Form		Name	Value	Num: value	Form		Name	Value	Num: value
Ⰰ	Ⰰ	Az	a	1	Ⱆ	Ⱆ	Uk	u	400
Ⰱ	Ⰱ	Buky	b	2	Ⰼ	Ⰼ	Fert	f, ph	500
Ⰲ	Ⰲ	Vědi	v	3	ⰶ	ⰶ	Chěr	kh (ch)	600
Ⰳ	Ⰳ	Glagol'	g	4	Ⱁ	Ⱁ	Ó	ó	700
Ⰴ	Ⰴ	Dobro	d	5	Ⱍ	Ⱍ	Šta	št	800
Ⰵ	Ⰵ	Est'	e	6	Ⱌ	Ⱌ	Ci	ts	900
Ⰶ	Ⰶ	Živěte	ž	7	Ⱎ	Ⱎ	Červ'	č	1000
Ⰷ	Ⰷ	Zělo	z	8	Ⱎ	Ⱎ	Ša	š	
Ⰸ	Ⰸ	Zemlja	z	9	ⱝ	ⱝ	} Jer	o	
Ⱑ	Ⱑ	Iže	i	10	Ⰺ	Ⰺ		o̅	
Ⰻ	Ⰻ	I	i	20	ⱝⰸ	ⱝⰸ	} Jery	y	
Ⱀⱃ	Ⱀⱃ	{ Děrv' { č. Jot	dy, y	30	ⱝⱜ	ⱝⱜ	} Jerek	e	
Ⱏ	Ⱏ	Kako	k	40	ⰺ	ⰺ		i̅	
Ⰾ	Ⰾ	Ljudi	l	50	Ⱐ	Ⱐ	Jet'	ě, ya	
Ⰿ	Ⰿ	Myslite	m	60	Ⱓ	Ⱓ	Ju	yu	
Ⱀ	Ⱀ	Naš	n	70	Ⱔ	Ⱔ	Ęs	ę	
Ⱁ	Ⱁ	On	o	80	Ⱗ	Ⱗ	As	ą	
Ⱂ	Ⱂ	Pokoj	p	90	Ⱘ	Ⱘ	Jęs	yę	
Ⱃ	Ⱃ	R'ci	r	100	Ⱙ	Ⱙ	Jąs	yą	
Ⱄ	Ⱄ	Slovo	s	200	Ⱚ	Ⱚ	Thita	th	
Ⱅ	Ⱅ	Tvr'do	t	300	Ⱛ	Ⱛ	Ižica	y	

NOTES.

1. These characters are designed to be printed without the abbreviations, peculiar to liturgical works.
2. The numerical letters are distinguished by dots on both sides, as .Ⰰ. .Ⰱ. etc.
3. The punctuation is the same as in other languages.
4. The letters Ⱔ, Ⱗ, Ⱘ and Ⱙ, the forms ⱝ and Ⰺ, together with the combinations ⱝⰸ and ⱝⱜ, are only found in Bulgarian MSS. The ligature Ⱎ instead of ⰶ only occurs in Croatian MSS.
5. The value and pronunciation of the accented Roman characters may be ascertained by referring to the Czechian and Polish Alphabets.

RUSSIAN

Form		Name	Value	Observations
Straight	Italic			
А а	*А а*	As	a	The Russian Alphabet consists of 35 letters. Ecclesiastical and Old-Russian works, being written in the ancient Slavonic character, contain the following additional letters, *ꙁ (Selo)* s, *ꙋ* or *ȣ (Ik)* u, *ѡ (Ot)* o, *ѫ (Yuss)* ю, *ꙍ (O)* ó, *ѯ (Ksi)* x, *ѱ (Psi)* ps. In ecclesiastical books these letters serve as numerals, and are arranged as in Greek. The sign ҃ is placed over numerical letters.
Б б	*Б б*	Buki	b	
В в	*В в*	Vyedi	v ff	
Г г	*Г г*	Glagol	g gh	
Д д	*Д д, д*	Dobro	d	
Е е	*Е е*	Yest	é yé yo o	
Ж ж	*Ж ж*	Zhivete	zh sh	
З з	*З з*	Zemla	z	
И Й и й	*И Й и й*	Izhe	i	a has the sounds of *bar* and *bat*.
I i ï	*I i ï*	I	i	б like *b*. Before the strong consonants and as a final letter it sounds like *p*.
К к	*К к*	Kako	k ck	в 1) At the beginning of a syllable and before л н р like *v*. 2) As a final, and before a hard consonant, like *ff*.
Л л	*Л л*	Lïudi	l	г 1) As an initial and medial letter nearly like *g* in *give*, but with a hard Hibernian aspiration. 2) As a final, or before *sh*, like *k*. 3) In ecclesiastical pronunciation it is aspirated like *h*. In some words, especially foreign, it sounds like *ch* in the Scotch *loch*. 4) The adjectival and pronominal ending ro is commonly pronounced *vo*, and in inferior style it is even spelled so.
М м	*М м*	Muislete	m	
Н н	*Н н*	Nash	n	
О о	*О о*	On	o a	
П п	*П п*	Pokoi	p	
Р р	*Р р*	Rtsui	r	
С с	*С с*	Slovo	s	
Т т m	*Т т m*	Tverdo	t	
У у	*У у*	U	u	д as our *d*.
Ф ф	*Ф ф*	Fert	ph f	е 1) At the beginning of syllables like *yai*. 2) At the end of syllables like *e* in *met*, with a feeble *y* before it. After sibilants this *y* is not heard. 3) When accented it sounds like *yeo* in *yeoman*, and after ж ч ш щ ц like *o* in *go*. This rule is applied *a)* before a consonant followed by the vowels *a, o, y*, ы, ъ; *b)* at the end of a word; *c)* in the instrumental case ею or ей of nouns fem. sing; *d)* before г, к, х, and the sibilants ж, ш. *e)* in the present tense. In improved spelling the sound of *yo* or *o* is indicated by ë. This ë also denotes the French sound of *eu*.
Х х	*Х х*	Kherr	kh (ch in Ger.)	
Ц ц	*Ц ц*	Tsui	ts	
Ч ч	*Ч ч*	Tsherv	ch	
Ш ш	*Ш ш*	Sha	sh	
Щ щ	*Щ щ*	Shtsha	shch	
Ъ ъ	*Ъ ъ*	Yerr	hard suffix	
Ы ы	*Ы ы*	Yerui	ui i thick	
Ь ь	*Ь ь*	Yer	soft suffix	
Ѣ ѣ	*Ѣ ѣ*	Yat	yé éyo	ж like *j* in the French word *jour*.
Э э	*Э э*	E	è	и and i sound alike.
Ю ю	*Ю ю*	Yu	yoo Fr.	
Я я	*Я я*	Ya	ya yè	
Ѳ ѳ	*Ѳ ѳ*	Fita	f	
Ѵ ѵ	*Ѵ ѵ*	Izhitza	y v	

RUSSIAN

Observations	CURRENT HAND			

The alphabet table (current hand cursive and printed forms):

𝒜 𝒜 α a	А а		𝒯𝒯 m m	Т т				
Б Б б б	Б б		𝒰 𝒰 у у	У у				
В В в в	В в		Ф Ф ф ф	Ф ф				
Г Г г г	Г г		Х Х х х	Х х				
Д Д g g	Д д		Ц Ц ц ц	Ц ц				
Е Е е е	Е е		Ч Ч ч ч	Ч ч				
Ж Ж ж ж	Ж ж		Ш Ш ш ш	Ш ш				
З З з з	З з		Щ Щ щ щ	Щ щ				
И И и и	И и		Ъ Ъ ъ ъ	Ъ ъ				
I I i i	I ï		Ы Ы ы ы	Ы ы				
К К к к	К к		Ь Ь ь ь	Ь ь				
Л Л л л	Л л		Ѣ Ѣ ѣ ѣ	Ѣ ѣ				
М М м м	М м		Э	э Э э				
Н Н н н	Н н		Ю Ю ю ю	Ю ю				
О О о о	О о		Я Я я я	Я я				
П П п п	П п		Ѳ Ѳ ѳ ѳ	Ѳ ѳ				
Р Р р р	Р р		Ѵ Ѵ ѵ ѵ	V ѵ				
С С с с	С с							

Observations (left column):

л final, attended by ъ, sounds very hard.

о accented, sounds like the o in go. When unaccented it is pronounced like the a in far.

х is a stronger guttural than ch in the Scotch loch.

ц like tz in Fritz.

ч ordinarily like ch in church. In что (what) and before n it takes the sound of sh.

щ consists of the sounds of sh-ch. A notion of its pronunciation may be formed by a connected articulation of the letters sh-chi in the words Engli**sh ch**ildren.

ъ after a final consonant produces a hard and ringing sound.

ь is placed at the end of words where it softens the preceding consonant, and adds to it the sound of ye, such as is heard in the French pronunciation of Charlemagne. In the middle of a word, mostly between two consonants, it is uttered with a slight sound of ee.

ы is identical with the Polish y, and somewhat like the English we, when rapidly articulated.

ѣ as an initial like yai. The y of this diphthong is also sounded in the middle of a syllable after n, but is scarcely audible after other consonants.

э This reversed e is the initial of words commencing with the sound ai. It occurs in foreign words in which it replaces oe.

ю sounds like ew. In foreign words it is similar to the French u.

я when accented, sounds like ya in yard. In unaccented initial syllables it sounds ye. After consonants it is pronounced like e in met. As a final letter it takes the sound of ya in yard.

ѳ represents the same Greek letter but is pronounced like F. In modern derivations from the Greek it is replaced by F.

ѵ only occurs in Greek words. At the beginning of a word or after a consonant it sounds like ee, and after a vowel like v.

The letters h, c, x, f, do not occur in the Russian alphabet. They are represented as follows: 1) h is replaced by г, as in Гамбургъ Hamburg, or it is omitted altogether, especially in Latin words as Аннибалъ, Hannibal. 2) c before e, i, y, sounding like the German z or tz, is expressed by ц as Цицеронъ, and before a, o, u by k, as Коллегія. 3) x is expressed by кс, as Алексѣй (Alexius). 4) f and the German v are changed into Ф, as Фридрихъ Frederick.

DIPHTHONGS.

Proper diphthongs are only formed by the a following a vowel. This letter receives in such a case a characteristic sign at the top (й). The diphthongs are

ай ей ій ой уй ый ѣй эй юй яй.

ACCENTS.

The stress of an accented vowel is indicated by the acute (´) and the grave (`). The former denotes the raising, the latter the depression of the tone. The accents are only then marked in writing, when corresponding forms are to be distinguished from one another. They are placed over the following vowels

а е и і о у ы ъ я ѵ.

SERVIAN.

(Modern form, cut by F. Rösch in Leipzic.)

This language is divided into the dialects of the Herzegovina, of Ressava and Syrmia. The Servians use the Slavonic (Cyrillic), the Croats and Wends the Roman characters.

Cyrillic	Latin	Pronunciation
А а	A a	a
Б б	B b	b
В в	V v	v
Г г	G g	g
Д д	D d	d
Ђ ђ	Dj dj	dy, Hungarian gy
Е е	E e	e
Ж ж	Ž ž	j in French
З з	Z z	z
И и	I i	i
І і	I i	y
Ј ј	J j	y
К к	K k	k
Л л	L l	l
Љ љ	Lj lj	ly, Ital. gl, gli
М м	M m	m
Н н	N n	n
Њ њ	Nj nj	ñ Ital. and Fr. ng
О о	O o	o
П п	P p	p
Р р	R r	r
С с	S s	s
Т т	T t	t
Ћ ћ	Ć ć	ty, lj
У у	U u	u
Ф ф	F f	f
Х х	H h	h
Ц ц	C c	ts
Ч ч	Č č	ch
Ш ш	Š š	sh
Щ щ	Šć šć	shch
Ъ ъ	—	hardening suffix
Ы ы	I i	ee, French ü
Ь ь	—	softening suffix
Ѣ ѣ	Je je ě ie	yé, ié
Є є	Je je	yé
Ю ю	Ju ju	yū
Я я	Ja ja	yä
Џ џ	Dž dž	j
Ѳ ѳ	Th th	th

ž like s in measure. dž like j in jar. r has the power both of a consonant and a vowel. As a consonant it sounds as in other languages. As a vowel it forms a separate syllable and is pronounced with a very slight sound of e. The orthography of this syllable varies. Some spell it er, the Ragusans ar. Others omit a and e and simply write r, others again write ŕ.

Accents used in Servian: acute (´); sign of length (´): ᴗ or ⌒ sign of brevity.

ILLYRIAN.

Nr. I represents the "organic" orthography now used in Roman-Catholic publications; Nrs. II and III are to some extent current in Slavonia, Croatia and Dalmatia.

I.	II.	III.	Pronunciation
a	a	a	The Vowels a, o, u, i, e sound as in German or Italian.
b	b	b	
c	c	cz	
ć	ch	ch	
č	cs	cs	ě as a medial, follows all the consonants except gutturals. It rarely is a final letter and never an initial. Its general sound is like ye (in yes). In the dialect of the Herzegovina it has the same pronunciation when not lengthened, otherwise it sounds like ee combined with ye, as is heard in see yet. Before i, like y in ye. In the Syrmian dialect it varies between ay and ee. In the Ressava dialect it almost invariably sounds like ay (in nay). This ě is now often spelled ie.
d	d	d	
dj	dj	dy	
e	e	e	
ě	e i	e i	
f	f	f	
g	g	g	
gj	gj	gy	
h	h	h	
i	i	i	
j	j	j	
k	k	k	
l	l	l	
lj	lj	ly	c is like ts in lots.
m	m	m	ć and tj almost like ts. The difference between these spellings is, that ć can be used indiscriminately, and tj only in derived words.
n	n	n	
nj	nj	ny	
o	o	o	
p	p	p	č like j in jar.
r	r	r	
s	s	ss sz	dj and gj are nearly like j in jar.
š	sh	sc	
t	t	t	lj like lli in William.
tj	ch	ty	
u	u	u	nj like ni in opinion.
v	v	v	
z	z	z	š like sh.
ž	x	s	
dž	dx cx	ds	

WALLACHIAN

Form	Name	Value
Я а	As	a
Б в	Buke	b
В в	Vide	v
Г г	Glagol	g
Д д	Dobro	d
Є є	Yest	ye e long
Ж ж	Shivete	zh
Ѕ ѕ	Zalo	Nr. 6
З з	Zemlia	z
И Й й	I	i
І ї ї	Ishe	y
К к	Kako	k
Л л	Lïude	l
М m	Meslite	m
Н н	Nash	n
О о	On	o
П п	Pokoi	p
Р р	Rtse	r
С с	Slovo	s
Т т	Tverdo	t
Ѹ ѻ	Uk	u
Оу оу	Uniku	u
Ф ф	Fert	f ph
Х х	Khir	kh h
Ѡ ѡ	O	O long
Ц ц	Tsi	ts
Ч ч	Cher	ch
Ш ш	Sha	sh
Щ щ	Shta	sht
Ъ ъ	Yor	e short
Ѣ ѣ	Yaty	éa
Ѫ ѫ	Yus	è (uüh)
Ю ю	Yu	yu
Я я	Yako	ya
Ꙗ ꙗ	Ia	ya
Ѳ ѳ	Ftita	ft th
Ѱ ѱ	Psi	ps
Ѯ ѯ	Xi	x
Ѵ ѵ	Ishitza	v i *
Ѧ ѧ	Ün	üng in Germ.
Ц ц	Je	j

Besides the Alphabet on the left there are two varieties of characters.

ь (pronounced *Eer*) is appended to a consonant at the end of a word without being sounded. In modern printing it is omitted.

ы (*Yory*) is only employed in words of Slavonic origin.

ѵ *Ishitza*, occurs in words derived from the Greek. After vowels its sound is в, after consonants i (as in *Bit*).

SHORT ACCENTS.

◌ is placed over an initial vowel and the diphthong ю.

◌ stands over a medial and final н and over a final ю.

LONG ACCENTS.

" over initial vowels and over ю.

' over medial vowels.

over the medial ѫ and the final а, ѣ, ѫ, н.

‾ ⌐ over abbreviations and letters employed as numerals.

Modern Shape

А	a	à
Б	б	b
В	в	v
Г	г	g
Д	д	d
Е	е	y
Ж	ж	zh
З	з	z
І	i	i
К	к	k
Л	л	l
М	м	m
Н	н	n
О	о	o
П	п	p
Р	р	r
С	с	s
Т	т	t
У	у	u
Ф	ф	f
Х	х	kh(ch)
Ц	ц	ts
Ч	ч	ch
Ш	ш	sh
Щ	щ	sht
Ъ	ъ	e
Ѣ	ѣ	éa
Я	я	ya
Ѫ	ѫ	(uüh)
Ѧ	ѧ	ün
Ц	ц	j

Ѩ and Ѵ are only used in foreign words.

Improved Modern Shape

Antiqua		Current		
A	a	A	a	a
Б	б	Б	б	b
B	ʙ	B	ʙ	v
B	в	B	в	g
Г	г	Г	г	g
D	d	D	d	d
E	e	E	e	yé e
Ɉ	ɉ	Ɉ	ɉ	j (Fr.)
Z	z	Z	z	z
I	i	I	i	i
K	k	K	k	k
L	л	L	л	l
M	m	M	m	m
N	n	N	n	n
O	o	O	o	o
П	п	П	п	p
P	p	P	p	r
S	s	S	s	s
T	t	T	t	t
Y	ү	Y	ү	u
Ф	ф	Ф	ф	f
X	x	X	x	kh(ch)
Ц	ц	Ц	ц	ts
Ч	ч	Ч	ч	ch
Ш	ш	Ш	ш	sh
Ъ	ъ	Ъ	ъ	e
Î	î	Î	î	(ün)
Ц	ц	Ц	ц	j

APOSTROPHISED LETTERS.

Ăă Ĕĕ Ĭĭ Ĭĭ Ŏŏ Y̆
Ŭŭ Dd Şş Tt Я'Я

The Alphabet to the left is used in liturgical and ancient works. With the improved cultivation of the language the letters have been considerably simplified, as is shown in the two Alphabets at the right. No notice has been taken here of the ancient names and the accentuation of the letters.

POLISH

a like	a
Ą ą —	ong
e —	e
é —	ié
Ę ę —	eng
i —	i
o —	o
Ó ó —	ou
u —	u
y —	e (ŭ)
b —	b
b́ —	by'
c —	ts
Ć ć —	tssh
cz —	ch
d —	d
dz —	dz
dź —	dzy'
dż —	j
f —	f
g —	g
h —	h (ch)
ch —	kh
j —	y
k —	k
l —	l
Ł ł —	—
m —	m
ḿ —	my'
n —	n
Ń ń —	ny'
p —	p
ṕ —	p
r —	r
rz —	rsh
s —	s
Ś ś —	sy'
sz —	sh
t —	t
w —	v
ẃ —	vy'
z —	z
Ż ż, —	zy'
Ż ż Ź ż —	j (Fr.)

The marginal column shows the pronunciation of Polish letters in as far as it approximates the English. The vowels *a, e, i, o, ou, u, ü* in the adjoining column are sounded as in German. The following peculiarities must be noticed.

In addition to the five elementary vowels, common to the European languages, occurs *y*, which is deeper than the *i* and sharper than the French mute *e* (in *poudre*, Polish *pudyr*). As accessory vowels of *a, e* stand the nasals *ą* and *ę (ong, eng)*. Before *b, p*, they sound *om*, but nasally; *é*, always strongly accented, is an intermediate of *e* and *i*. In *ie, ia, io, iu* the *i* merely indicates the softness of the preceding consonant; in fact this *i* forms part of such a consonant. *ó* is a strongly accented deep *o*, nearly like *u*. Hence the Polish vowels descend in the following gradation: *i, é, (ie), e, ę, y, a, ą, o, ó, u*.

These vowels have a clear and distinct sound, except the *i* which obtains the consonantal force of *y*, when it is followed by a vowel and preceded by *b, c, dz, m, n, p, s, w, z*. In this case the *i* is merely the medium of softening the consonant, Ex: *biodro* (loin) sounds *byodro*. Before *e* it becomes *ie*.

The consonants *b́, ć, dź, ḿ, n, p, s, w, z* are attended by a slight and rapid articulation of *y*, as if written *by, cy, dzy, my, ny, py, sy, wy, zy*. They stand as finals of words, and also of syllables followed by consonants. Of these letters *ć* takes the intermediate sound of our *h* and *ch*.

c sounds like *ts* in *wants*.

cz is our *ch*, and *sz* our *sh*.

dz sounds like *ds* in *wands*.

dż is like *j* in *jar*.

h is of rare occurrence, the Slavonic *h* being represented in Polish by *g*. It is as guttural as the German *ch*, Ex: *hultaj* (a Good for nothing).

ł the virgulated *l* is heavier than the common *l*. The middle part of the tongue is more raised in the articulation of this letter.

rz is *r* blended with *ż*. The *r* is softly rolled, and its *z* is like the French *j*. Ex: *przy*.

ż like *j* in the French word *jour*.

To avoid the accumulation of softening *iota*-marks of the letters *b́, ḿ, ń, ṕ, ś, ẃ, ż*, the following process is preferred. Before a vowel an *i* is inserted (as *bia mia* etc.); before *i* however and before consonants the *iota*-sign is dispensed with; *b́, ṕ, ẃ, ḿ*, lose this sign even at the end of a word. Owing to the diminution of the characteristic signs, the letters *w, b, p, m, n, s, z* deviate from the original rule and may be followed by either *i* or *y*.

SORBIAN or WENDISH OF LUSATIA.

The vowels are: a, o, u, y, e, i. The union of a and o makes ò; o and u form ó; e and i coalesce in è. The semi-consonant j is connected with i; h with e; w with a o u.

The consonants are divided 1) into Labials w, f, v, b, p, m. 2) Palatals and Linguals n, l, r. 3) Dentals d, t, ć. 4) Sibilants z ź, s ś, c č. 5) Gutturals h ch (g) k.

With regard to their articulation these consonants are divided into broad and slender sounds, according as they are hardened or softened in their utterance.

Broad sounds: w, ẃ, b, b́, z, ź, d, dz, dź, h, g.

Slender sounds: f, v, p, ṕ, s, ś, t, c, ó, č, ds, ts, ch, k.

Between these letters nine intermediates take their place: m, ḿ, n, ń, l', l, ł, r, ŕ.

The whole Alphabet thus consists of the following 8 vowels and 32 consonants. A (ò) o, ó, u, y, e, e, i; j, w, ẃ (f, v) b, b́, p, ṕ, m, ḿ, n, ń, ł, l, (l'), r, ŕ, z, ź, s, ś, d, dz, dź, t, c, ć, č, ts, h, ch, g, k.

In combining one consonant or several consonants with a vowel to form a syllable, a distinction is made between hard soft and neutral consonants.

At the same time the following rule is to be observed. In the grammatical combinations of structure, derivation, declension, comparison and conjugation the vowel y cannot follow a soft consonant, nor can e and i follow a hard consonant, whilst the neutral consonants may be succeeded by either y or i. In conformity with this rule are reckoned as

Soft, j ẃ v b́ ṕ ḿ ń l ŕ ź ś ć dź č.

Hard, ł r z s d dz t c (h ch g k).

Neutral, w f b p m n ds ts.

The letters qu and x, in words of foreign origin, are spelled kw and ks, as kwadrat, Aleksander, kwas. Also g occurs only in foreign words. V and f are found in but few vernacular terms.

PRONUNCIATION OF THE CONSONANTS.

The accented characters ẃ b́ ṕ ḿ ń ŕ differ from the unaccented in softness of sound. Before e (acute) è and i this accent is unnecessary, because these vowels are sufficient to soften the preceding consonants.

ł sounds like v. In the north-eastern part of the country it is pronounced like a harsh l. For instance čóło.

dz as in English, but without a break between the two letters. Example na fidzy.

dź like g in gentle, as dźera, nadźya.

z as in English, f. i. zuby.

ź like the s in pleasure, f. i. żolty.

ś like sh, f. i. šaty, šéry.

c like ts, as cybać.

ó nearly like ch in churn, f. i. óerń.

č the sharpest sibilant like tch in wretch, f. i. čoruy.

ds, ts like ts, f. i. tsihuó.

ch is frequently pronounced hard, like c before a, o, u, especially at the beginning of words, for instance chory.

j like y in yes.

s like z.

w like v.

PRONUNCIATION OF THE VOWELS.

a i u as the vowels in are, here, true.

e is acute, grave, or long. After c z s it is often pronounced like y.

o acute grave or lengthened.

ó deep nearly like u.

è like ea in dear.

y deep as ea in dearth.

CZECHIAN or BOHEMIAN.

Roman.

a b c d e f g h ch i j k l m n o p r s t u v y z — á é í ú ý — u — ě

Č č Ď ď D' ď' Ǧ ǧ ň Ř ř Š š Ť ť ľ Ž ž

German.

a b c d e f g h ch i j k l m n o p r ſ s t u v y z — á é í ú ý — ú — ě

Č č Ď ď D' ď' G ǧ ň Ř ř Š ſ š Ť ť ľ Ž ž

q and x only occur in foreign words. qu is generally replaced by kv as kvitance (receipt). Some writers use w for v and ou for au.

The accented vowels á é í ú y and ů are long; without accent their pronunciation is short.

ě i í are termed soft vowels. The others are hard.

h ch k r are hard consonants.

c č d' j ň ř š ť ž are soft, and

b d f g l m n p s t v z are called indednite consonants.

THE FOLLOWING SOUNDS DIFFER FROM THE ENGLISH PRONUNCIATION.

a sounds like the first a in papa.

á like a in father.

c even before k, sounds like ts, as necky (nets-ku) the tray.

č like ch in church.

d before i í or when marked with the liquifying sign (d') is sounded dy. This consonantal y is softly blended with its d, as div or diw (pronounced dyiv).

e like e in den.

é like a in late.

ě as ye in yet. It can only occur after v, f, b, p, m, n, d, t with which it coalesces. As věk (vyek) a century.

ey like a in late followed by y in yet, as woley (call thou). This final y forms a distinct sound.

g as in garnet. It only occurs in foreign words.

h aspirated at the beginning and in the middle of a word like h in house. At the end of a syllable it partakes of the guttural sound of ch and is somewhat softer than ch in the Scotch loch.

ch like ch in the Scotch word loch, as chleb (bread).

i as in grin.

í like ee in green.

j like y, as jaro (pr. yaro) springtime.

n before i í, or when marked ň, sounds like ni in opinion.

o as in of.

ó as in door.

ou is a diphthong which blends the sound of o (in pole) with u (in put). These vowels retain their separate pronunciation in verbs with prefixed po, as poubrati (po - u - bra - ti).

š (in German type ſſ, and as a final, š) like sh in fish.

t before i í, or when marked ť, sounds like a t with which the semi-vowel y coalesces, as ľulipan (pron. tyoo - le - pan) tulip.

u as in put.

ú and ů long as in blue.

y like u in the French pure.

z as in English but.

ž like s in measure.

ORTHOEPIC RULES.

1) The vowels with the long accent (´) should not be lengthened to excess.

2) The consonants š, ž, z, ž, become mute before the affix sky, as vesský.

3) The consonant j, as an initial before another consonant, is not pronounced, as jsem. When a syllable ending in a vowel precedes, the j becomes audible.

4) The compounds tc ds and ts are pronounced like c; dš and tš, like č.

5) Prepositions consisting of a simple consonant, such as k, s, v, z, although standing by themselves, do not form a syllable, but are sounded together with the first syllable of the next word, for instance k tobě s námi. These unconnected prepositions cannot be placed by themselves at the end of a line or a page.

6) The auxiliary verb. jsem, jsi, jest-jsme, jste, jsou, the conjunctional particles bych, bys, by, bychom, byste, bý, and the reflective pronouns se, si attached to an active participle, are blended together in the pronunciation and joined by a hyphen. The same is the case when si, se are postpositions of nouns or adjectives. E. g. shledání-se, modlíci-se.

7) The soft consonants must be carefully distinguished in articulation from the indefinites, and the i i ů must properly coalesce with the latter.

8) The sibilants c s z differ from each other as well as from č š ž.

9) h is never mute. Example hrom (thunder) in which the h sounds as the h in the Scotch pronunciation of which.

10) The accent always rests on the first syllable, as be-žím, pri-nesu. The accented syllable may at the same time be lengthened, as sná-žím, krá-sa.

DIVISION OF SYLLABLES.

In words which are difficult to pronounce, owing to the complication of consonants, it is of importance to ascertain the component syllables. In this language most syllables end in vowels. The following circumstances must be noticed in applying this rule.

1) A consonant placed between two vowels or between a vowel and l or r, joins the next syllable. Example: stra-kn, ba-vl-na.

2) Of several consonants, followed by a vowel, only the last consonant goes to the next syllable; yet sk, šk, st, št are not separated but join the next syllable. In such instances the preceding syllable is often without a vowel, while l or r forms the medial consonant. Example, hrn-číř.

3) l, r, ř, with a vowel after, are joined by the preceding consonant in forming one syllable. To this rule n forms an exception. The consonants sk, šk, st, št must without separation be annexed to the syllable which follows. Example, kno-flík, zei-dlik, svě-tlo, han-li-vý.

4) Compound words are divided according to their component parts, as ou-voz, ná-dvo-ří.

HUNGARIAN.

The Hungarian language comprises 31 sonants which are expressed by the Roman Alphabet. Owing to the combinations of some letters the Alphabet is formed as follows:

a b cs cz d e f g gy h i j k l ly m n ny o ö p r s sz t ty u ü v z zs.

The vowels a e i o ö u ü, are sounded as in German. With the accent at the top the vowels á é í ó ő ú ű are lengthened.

The combinations cs cz gy ly ny sz ty zs represent single articulations and are inseparable in spelling.

cs	sounds like	ch as	kocsi.
cz	»	» ts as	czukor.
gy	»	» di in the French word Dieu, as	gyár.
ly	»	» il in the French word email, as	homály.
ny	»	» ni in opinion, as	anya.
sz	»	» s as	szag.
ty	»	» ti in the French metier as	tyuk.
zs	»	» j in the French word jour as	zsák.

With regard to the consonants is to be noticed that,

j is pronounced like y in yes, and
s like the English sh, as sas.

The letters c ch q w x are only found in foreign words, for instance Cato, Achilles.

y does not represent an independent sound, but simply helps to soften the antecedent letter. Nevertheless in Old-Hungarian words y and ch are employed as independent letters. The former then sounds like i in it, and ch as in church. For example Pálffy, Forgach.

The compounds cs and cz are often denoted by ts and tz. Modern Orthography rejects this spelling except in words where the t is radical, as barátság (not barácság).

LETTISH.

The Lets have adopted the following 22 letters of the German Alphabet,

a b c d e g h i j k l m n o p r s t u w z.

The c and h are only used in combination with s to express the sounds of sch and sch. The h moreover serves to lengthen the vowels. The German consonants h ch f v never occur in Lettish. Nor are ö and ü in use. The q x y are represented by fw, ts, i.

By means of the 22 characters the following 34 simple sounds of the Lettish language are formed.

a b bj d c g g G j i k k K l l L m mj n n N o p p pj r r R s bs sch dsch f S (s) sch t tsch u w wj z.

PRONUNCIATION OF THE SIMPLE VOWELS.

a e i u are short. When lengthened they are marked thus,

â ê î û

The o is always long, nevertheless it receives the lengthening mark to distinguish the accented oh and ö from the lighter o.

PRONUNCIATION OF THE DIPHTHONGS.

There are six diphthongs in this language, ai au ei oi ui ee. The first five are pronounced as in German. Although ai and ei are naturally long they occur with the circumflex âi êi. The diphthong oi only appears in the word woi. When au and ui are to become separate syllables the u and i are marked with the diaeresis, aü, uï. Peculiar is the sound of ee; it passes from the articulation of ee (such as is heard in the German word See or in the English word say) to an intermediate sound, such as is heard in the second a of advantage.

CONSONANTS.

The following letters have the English sound, b d f m n p r t. The j is a consonant like our y; w sounds as v, and z like ts. The labials b m p w may be followed by the modifying j, which like the Russian ь, helps to soften the consonant and causes a slight i to ring after it. It cannot be separated from the consonant nor uttered as an independent letter. l n r are virgulated as l n r, instead of being followed by j. Besides these letters the following four are virgulated.

g like the German k before e and i; g is like k before a o u.

k hard like k in king, k as c in come, cut.

f, sharp like our s. s is the final of this sharp f.

s is soft like our z.

bs form an inseparable sound like the soft Italian z.

sch sharp like the Russian ш and the English sh. The virgula of s and sch does not indicate the sound of an inherent j. It only helps to distinguish the sharply pronounced consonant from the soft s and sch, the latter is pronounced like the Russian ж or the French j in jour.

tsch is like the English ch and dsch like g in gentle.

PRONUNCIATION OF SUCCESSIVE CONSONANTS.

Two or more Consonants, joined together in one syllable or in two syllables, must be so articulated that each should retain its original and independent sound. The n is somewhat modified with the g and k. It being assimilated with these letters, its sound is like that in the English words sing, sink (not as in tingle, tinkle). When g and k are marked with the cross-stroke the n is likewise virgulated, and is then pronounced in accordance with the foregoing rules.

GERMAN

𝒶		𝔄	a	a	𝒩		ℜ	n	n	𝔄̈	Ä ä ä
		𝔅	b	b			𝔇	o	o		Ö ö ö
		ℭ	c	c			𝔓	p	p		Ü ü ü
		𝔇	d	d			𝔔	q	q		ch
		𝔈	e	e			ℜ	r	r		ck
		𝔉	f	f			𝔖 ſ	s	s		ff
		𝔊	g	g			𝔗	t	t		ti
		ℌ	h	h			𝔘	u	u		fl
		ℑ	i	i			𝔙	v	v		ſi
		ℑ	j	j			𝔚	w	w		ss
		ℜ	k	k			𝔛	x	x		ſt
		ℒ	l	l			𝔜	y	y		sz
		𝔐	m	m			ℨ	z	z		tz

The vowels are: a ä e i o ö u ü. The diphthongs or compound vowels are: ai ei au äu eu; all other letters are consonants.

Simple vowels.

Every vowel, followed by two consonants, is short, if followed by only one consonant it is long.

𝔄 a is pronounced like *a* in the English word *father*.
𝔄 ä is pronounced like *a* in the English word *late*.
ℭ e is pronounced like *e* in the English word *let*.
ℑ i is pronounced like *e* in the English word *me*.
𝔇 o is pronounced like *o* in the English word *hope*.
𝔇 ö is pronounced like *eu* in the French word *seul*.
𝔘 u is pronounced like *oo* in the English word *roof*.
𝔘 ü is pronounced like the French *u*. There is no corresponding sound in the English language.
𝔜 y has the sound of the German i, by which it is generally replaced.

Double vowels.

The double vowels aa, ee, oo, are no diphthongs, because only one letter is sounded, and the second serves to indicate that the syllable is long.

ie is pronounced like *ee* in the English word *meat*.

Diphthongs.

In the German diphthongs, the two vowels must be sounded one after the other, but so quickly as to form only one syllable.

ai and ei are pronounced almost alike, and have the sound of the English *i* in the word *fire*.
au is pronounced like *ou* in the English word *house*.
äu and eu sound almost like *oy* in the word *joy*.

Consonants.

The pronunciation of the consonants differs but little in the two languages; the learner should notice the following peculiarities.

ℭ c before ä e and i is pronounced like *ts*.
Before a o u, before a consonant, and at the end of a syllable it is pronounced like *k*, by which in most cases it may be replaced.
ℭh at the beginning of a word is pronounced like *k*, except in words derived from the French, in which it retains the French pronunciation.

In the middle or at the end of a word ch has a pronunciation quite peculiar to the German language, and more or less guttural, but for which no corresponding sound can be found in English; it is like the Scotch *ch* in the word *loch* after a e u au, but softer after ä e i ö ü äu eu, and after a consonant.
chs or chſ is pronounced like *x* when these consonants belong to the root or radical syllable.
But the ch preserves its guttural pronunciation, when it stands before the *s* or *ſ* by contraction or in a compound word.
𝔊 g at the beginning of a syllable is pronounced like the English *g* in the word *good*; but between two vowels, in the middle of a word and at the end of a syllable it has a sound like the ch, only much softened.
After n at the end of a word it is pronounced like a very soft *k*.
ℌ h is always aspirated at the beginning of a syllable. The aspiration becomes however almost imperceptible before a final *e*.
After a vowel or a t, the h is not pronounced, but, only indicates that the syllable is long.
ℑ j only stands at the beginning of a syllable and is pronounced like the English *y* in the word *yet*.
d replaces the double *t*, and is pronounced short.
ℜu qu has the sound of *kv* in English.
𝔖 ſ s at the beginning of a syllable is pronounced like the English *z*, at the end of a syllable however like the English *s*.
The long ſ is placed at the beginning and in the middle, s only at the end of syllables. If in an uninflected word there are two ſ one after another, they are written ß.
ß is only placed at the end or in the middle of syllables, has the sound of the English *ss*.
ℭch ſch is pronounced like the English *sh*.
ſt and ſp are pronounced like *st* and *sp* in English; but in some parts of Germany they pronounce ſt at the beginning of a word like *sht*, and ſp like *shp*.
𝔚 v w is pronounced like the English *v*.
𝔛 x is sounded like *ts*.
ß replaces the double ſ and is pronounced very hard.

DANISH

𝔄 a	
𝔄a aa	
𝔅 b	
ℭ c	
𝔇 d	
𝔈 e	
𝔉 f	
𝔊 g	
ℌ h (haa)	
𝔍 i	
𝔍 j (Jod)	
𝔎 k (kaa)	
𝔏 l	
𝔐 m	
𝔑 n	
𝔒 o	
𝔓 p	
𝔒 q	
𝔑 r	
𝔖 ſ s	
𝔗 t	
𝔘 u	
𝔙 v (we)	
𝔛 x	
𝔜 y	
𝔷 z	
𝔚 æ (ä)	
𝔇 ø (ö)	

The Danish language forms part of the great Gothic family and derives its origin from the ancient Norse which once extended over the whole of Scandinavia. Hence it is closely connected with modern Icelandic and Swedish, more distantly with the German, Dutch and English languages. In its further development it has embodied a variety of terms from the French, Latin and Greek.

The Alphabet consists of the adjoining 28 characters.

VOWELS AND DIPHTHONGS.

The simple vowels are

a aa e i o u y æ ø

They are long as in Stat (the a as in star) Raad, Been, blid, or short as in Stab, Land, ved, Bib. The vowels e i o u y ø have an open sound as in Plet, Digt, gobt, or a close sound as in streb, strib, gob. e i u, as long middle vowels, are doubled unless the word ends in b d g v, as Steen, Been, Minus. At the end only the e is doubled, as see, see. The other vowels at the end of a syllable are always long, as Taa, Sti, Klo, and often add a mute e, as staae. In inflections the reduplication of the vowel ceases, as Huns, Huse. The vowels æ ø cannot be spelled ae oe. y is pronounced like the French u, not like the English y. Ex: Jube. aa mostly sounds like a in warm. In modern times å has been adopted for aa, and ö for the open ø. For the deep pronunciation of this vowel, the mark ø has been retained.

As diphthongs are reckoned ai ei oi øi au eu ou ui. Some grammarians only admit the following six, ai au ei eu ou øi. The pronunciation of these vowels consists in a rapid blending of their respective sounds.

CONSONANTS.

The consonants are

b c d f g h j k l m n p q r s t v x z.

According to the organs of speech they are divisible into: 1) Linguals d t l n r. 2) Labials b p v f m. 3) Palatals g k j. 4) Sibilants s z. 5) Aspirate h. In the dialect of the Juts the h is aspirated before j and v. b d g and v are softened to such a degree as to become frequently inaudible. After a vowel or when placed between two vowels d is pronounced dh (like the Anglo-Saxon ð or the English th in smooth). Double d has a similar pronunciation. ld and nd sound like ll and nn. In rd the d has a very soft sound. Also before ß the d loses part of its force, and it becomes inaudible before t. j sounds like y in yes. v sounds like the English w.

The following letters are peculiar to foreign words. 1) c before a o u or a consonant, is pronounced as in English; before e i y æ ø, it is like s. ch is like k. 2) q, followed by v, sounds like kv. 3) z is like dz or tz, and sometimes like the English z. 4) x in the middle and at the end of a word is like gs or ks. As an initial it is almost as soft as z.

Combinations of letters, ff ft fl ll ff st st ft.

SWEDISH.

Aa Bb Cc Dd Ee Ff Gg Hh Ii Jj Kk Ll Mm Nn Oo
Pp Qq Rr Ss Tt Uu Vv Xx Yy Zz Åå Ää Öö.

PRONUNCIATION OF THE VOWELS.

The vowels *a o u å* are hard, and *e i y ä ö* are soft. The vowels *a i u* sound as in German or Italian. *ä* is like *a* in *bare*. *å* like *o* in *tone*. The *e* sounds as *a* in *ale*. 1) when forming an independent syllable, Ex: *e-vig* (eternal). 2) at the end of a syllable, Ex: *ande* (spirit). 3) In many monosyllabic words, inflections, derivations and compounds. *e* sounds like *ai* in *air*. 1) before *f g l m n r*, when the next syllable of the same word is a consonant, as *efter* (after). 2) before *j* as *nej* (no). 3) in many monosyllables, as *elg* (elk). These rules have many exceptions. *o* has two sounds, 1) nearly as in *move*, when it constitutes a syllable by itself, or at the end of a word; also before the radical *m*, in nouns and adjectives; in all derivatives of words ending in *o*; before *x* and in various other forms of words. 2) *o* has a lengthened sound before a final *f*, and a sharp sound (as in *not*) before *m n p r t*. — *ö* is mostly lengthened (nearly like the French *eu* in *leur*) as *dö* (to die), or the sound is sharper and quicker, as *för* (for).

There are no diphthongs in this language.

CONSONANTS.

b retains its ordinary sound.

c before *k* stands for *kk*. Before *h* it only occurs in the Swedish word *Och* (pronounced *ock*). Before the soft vowels it sounds like *s*, before the hard vowels like *k*.

d sounds like our *d*. Before *t* like *t*. As a final after *n* almost like *n*. Before *j* it is silent.

f as in English. At the end of a word like *v*. In the middle of a word before *v* of the same syllable, also after *l* and *r*, it is mute. Ex: *kalfven* (pron. *kalven*). *f* and *v* of separate syllables retain their original sounds. Ex: *drifved* (= *driv - ved*).

g 1) as in *good* before a hard vowel, before *i* and *e* in a sharp unaccented syllable, at the end, and before a consonant of the same syllable. 2) like *y* in *yes*, before the soft vowels, and after *l* and *r*. Ex: *ge* (like *ya*). Of this rule there are some exceptions. 3) like *ck* when a *t* follows. Ex: *sagt* (=*sackt*). 4) like *ng* when a syllable ends in *gn*, as *vagn* (pronounced *vangn*). 5) before *j* it is mute. Ex: *gjort* (pr. *jort*).

h is aspirated, before *j* and *v* it is mute.

j like *y* in *yes*. After *f m n p* the *j* is clearly articulated and the preceding consonant has a very slight pronunciation. As a final letter it is somewhat like the German *ch*.

k 1) as in English. It is subject to the same rules as *g*. 2) before the soft vowels it is like our *ch*. In *kjortel* the *k* sounds like *t*.

l before *j* is mute.

m as in English. The final *m* sounds like two *m* in those radical words which, on being inflected, are spelled with double *m*. Ex: *lam* (pron. *lamm*).

q with *v* after, sounds like *kv*.

r and *s* as in English. *stj, sj, skj* like *sh*. *sk* before soft vowels is likewise pronounced as *sh*.

t as in English. *tj* like *ch* in *church*. *tion*, with a hard vowel before it, like *schone*, and after a consonant like *shone*.

v as in English. The word *von* is pronounced *fon* as in German from which language it is borrowed.

x is like *ks*.

z is pronounced like *s*.

ANGLO-SAXON.

The Anglo-Saxon language developed itself from the Low-German (Old-Saxon) idiom, which was introduced in England by the Saxons in or before the fifth century. In the ninth century this language was cultivated in writing, and obtained currency through the agency of laws and translations. In the eleventh century, with the overthrow of the Saxon dynasty and the commencement of the Norman rule, French became the language of the court and of judicial proceedings. The knowledge of the Anglo-Saxon language was confined to the dependent classes and to the residents of convents. In the thirteenth century, when this idiom once more became popular, it had received such an amount of foreign elements, and had lost so many native characteristics, that it could only be considered as a mixed dialect, out of which the modern English language was gradually formed.

	PRONUNCIATION.
A a a	a e i o u have the same sound as in German or Italian.
B b b	y has the same force as in English.
C c c	æ sounds as a in that.
D ð d	
E e e	
F ꝼ f	The Consonants have the following peculiarities of pronunciation.
G ȝ g	c is in all instances hard like k. cw stands for kw.
h h h	f between two vowels or as a final letter is pronounced like v.
I i i	g is always like the modern g in go. Occasionally ȝ occurs instead of g. This letter takes the sound of y in yes.
k k k	
L l l	
ꟙ m m	cg is used instead of gg.
N n n	h is a strong aspirate. As a final of a syllable and before a consonant it resembles the German ch.
O o o	
P p p	
R ꞃ r	
S ꞅ s	hw answers to the English wh. h is also found before the liquids l, n, r.
T c t	
U u u	w sometimes precedes r and l.
V ꝥ v	þ (tha) hard, like th in thick.
X x x	ð (eth) soft, like th in this. Usually þ is the initial and ð the final of a syllable.
Y y y	
Z z z	ꝸ and **F** stands for and.
Ð ð dh	þ̄ stands for þæt.
þ þ th	Ꝼ stands for oððe.

The accent (´) over a vowel denotes its length. In words of equal spelling this accent points out the difference of sound and meaning. For instance ác (but, ekr) ác (oak). The elision of m and n is indicated by a short line (˜) over the antecedent letter.

IRISH.

It has been a subject of learned discussions whether the Irish in the Pagan period made use of the ancient alphabets, which are known by the name of *Ogham*, and are preserved in some sculptured monuments and in various MSS. With the introduction of Christianity and the spreading of conventual education the subjoined Alphabet was formed, which is still employed in antiquarian publications and in some works intended for the Irish people. At the present time the Irish language is frequently written and printed in Roman (English) characters.

𝔞	ᴀ	a	2ꟙ	ꟃ	m
B	b	b	N	ꞑ	n
C	c	c k	O	o	o
Ꝺ	ᴆ	d	P	p	p
e	e	e	R	ꞃ	r
ꝼ	ꝼ	f	S	ꞅ	s
ᴣ	ᴣ	g	**C**	c	t
J	ᴊ	i	U	ᴜ	u
l	l	l	**h**	ꜧ	h

LIGATURES.

Irish MSS. contain contractions of which the following are the most usual.

ꝼ̃	chd		ꝫ	gh
ᴀᴅ	adh		ꞙᴏ, ꞙᴣ	i
ᴀᴇ	e		ꞁꞧ	ll
ꝗ	air		ꟃb	m
ꝓ	an		ꟃꞃ	m
ꝓ	am		ꟃ̇	w
⁊	agur		ꞁꝺ	n
ꝗ	ar		ꞙꞧ	nn
ꝧ	v w		ꝓ̇	f
bꞃ	v w		ꝓꝓ	b
bꝏ	b		ꞁꞧ	rr
cc	g		ꞃ̇	h
ċ	ch		ꞑ̇	si
ᴏꝼ	d		c̣	h
cc	d		cꞃ	t
ꝗ	ea		cc	d
ꝗᴅ	ea		ꞙ́	i
ꝼ̇	h		ꞙꝺ	i
ᴣc	g		ꞙꝺꞇ	ie
			ꟃ̇ᴣ	i

GOTHIC

Form	Value	Num: power	Ligatures and marks	Observations
ᚨ	a	1	**LIGATURES** of frequent occurrence in the Skeireins.	The Gothic language was in ancient times spoken by the eastern Germans who were designated by the collective name of Goths. It belongs to the Indo-Germanic family, and as a dead language, it has been remarkably preserved in the most ancient relic of Germanic literature. It is the first of the sister-languages that was committed to writing, and has thus reached us in its original purity. Although the relics of Gothic literature are very scanty, for beyond the fragmentary version of the Bible and the so called *Skeireins*, we possess but insignificant remains, there is enough matter extant to afford a perfect insight into the grammatical structure of the language.
B	b	2		
Γ	g	3		
ᚦ	d	4	Ꚋ for ʜT	
Ɵ	e	5	ᛗᛗ — ᚾᚨ	
ᚢ	q	6	ᛗᚾ — ᚾᚾ	
Z	z	7	ᚱᚴ — ᚾᚴ	
ʜ	h	8	ᚾᚾ — ᚾᚾ	
ψ	dh (þ)	9	ᚾᚨ — ᚾᚨ	
ιϔ	i	10	ᚾS — ᚾS	The Gothic Alphabet has the adjoining 25 letters. Their names are not known, as the language was not cultivated by native grammarians. The invention of the Gothic characters is attributed to Ulphilas.
ᚱ	k	20	ᚴψ — ᚴψ	
ᚺ	l	30	ᚴ $ — ψᚴ	
ᛗ	m	40		
N	n	50		
G	j	60	**MONOGRAMS.**	To distinguish the numerical letters from the other characters, the sign ⌐ or ⌐ is placed above or below the number. In these cases the diæresis over the ï is omitted. Such letters receive a characteristic dot on the right and left. In the Neapolitan copy two dots, in the shape af a colon, are placed on both sides of the letter. Instead of dots the upright circumflex is *l* sometimes to be found,
ᚢ	u	70	ᛗ̈	
Π	p	80	for matþaius	
ᚴ	r	100		
S	s	200	ᛗ̈	
T	t	300	for markus.	
Ϋ	v	400		·ʙ· (2), ːʜː (40), ʏGʏ (60).
Ϝ	f	500	**NUMERICAL FIGURES.**	The "catchword" is likewise enclosed between upright circumflexes, as ʏƟʏ.
X	x	600		## ORTHOGRAPHICAL SIGNS.
Ɵ	w	700	Ꚋ = 90	1. Diacritical signs only occur in the diæresis over the initial Ï.
Q	o	800	ᚷ = 900	

2. **Punctuation.** As a general rule the single stop represents the brief pause, and the double stop a longer pause. Yet this punctuation is not consistently carried out, such signs being often introduced without purpose, and contrary to the sense. After a long pause a blanc space is left. In the other parts of the text the words are all strung together without division, and sometimes the new sentence is placed in an other line, in which case the initial letters are preceded by the sign ⌐⌐ or ⌐⌐.

3. **The division of a word**, written in two lines, is often made without any rule, and merely to fill the vacant space. The separation is in rare instances indicated by a hyphen, which then is marked at the beginning of the new line, and not at the end of the preceding one.

4. **Quotations** are distinguished from the text by the single upright mark ʏ or the double ʏʏ. This mark is continued in the margin before all the lines which contain the quotation.
In the **Skeireins**, which has single marks of quotation, the sign ⌐⌐ is superadded in the first line, and the sign ⌐⌐ in the last.

5. **Abbreviations.** The elision of *n* is marked by ⌐ or ⌐, and *m* by ⌐ or ⌐. These signs are generally used at the end of a line, when there is not enough space for the letters, but sometimes they also occur in the middle of a line. Real abbreviations are in some instances indicated by the sign ʏ before and after the word, but generally the signs ⌐, ⌐ or ⌐ are employed.

RUNES

Form	Name	Value	Num: power
ᚠ	Fé	f	1
ᚢ	Ur	u	2
ᚦ	Thurs	th	3
ᚬ	Os	o	4
ᚱ	Reid	r	5
ᚴ	Kaun	k	6
ᚼ	Hagl	h	7
ᚾ	Naud	n	8
ᛁ	Is	i	9
ᛅ	Ar	a.	10
ᛋ	Sol	s	11
ᛏ	Tyr	t	12
ᛒ	Biörk	b	13
ᛚ	Laugr	l	14
ᛘ	Madr	m	15
ᛦ	Yr	y	16

Observations

The adoption of the Norse Runes takes its origin in remote antiquity, and probably belongs to a pre-christian period, as is suggested by a variety of coincidences, although hitherto no positive proofs have been discovered in the Runic stones, by which those monuments might be connected with the prevalence of paganism. As is the case in the Greek, Gothic and other alphabets, the Runic signs represent both letters and numerals. These characters, 16 in number, bear peculiar names, and appear to have been arranged in an arbitrary manner, no attention having been paid to the mutual relation and transition of the several letters.

The Runic characters were divided into three classes, in which the letter ᚠ headed the first series, ᚼ and ᛏ each of the other two series. These three divisions were therefore respectively named *Freys-aett* (Frey's family), *Hagls-aett* and *Tyrs-aett*. It is obvious that these letters could but imperfectly express the variety of sounds. There was only one sign for *g* and *k*, *d* and *t*, *b* and *p*, *u v* and *y*. It is most curious that the connective *e* and *ö* are omitted in this system. The latter vowel is replaced by *au*, and the former by *i*, *a*, *ia* and *ai*. Instead of *g* and *gh* the *h* is occasionally employed, while *u* might serve as the substitute of *o*, of the vowel *y*, of the diphthongs *ae*, *au* and *ey*, and even of the consonants *v* and *f*. *Yr* was equivalent to final *r* (of the same value as *or* and *ur*), and as such it was called *aur*. When the insufficiency of the Runic alphabet was more sensibly felt, four additional letters were adopted, namely *e*, *g*, *p* and *v*. Their names were no longer in conformity with the 16 archaic characters. Nor were new shapes given to these Runes. The simple expedient of adding one dot or two to the kindred letter was considered sufficient; therefore these sign bear the name of *stungnar runir* (dotted runes). The old letters adapted to this purpose are *i*, *k*, *b* and *f*. When the Roman characters, along with the use of paper and parchment were adopted in the North, the Runes were increased by the addition of *dh*, *d*, *ae*, *oe*, *ue*, and subsequently by the superfluous letters *c*, *q*, *x* and *z*. The latter signs may be regarded as spurious augmentations of the Runes. The same criticism seems to hold good in reference to the three double runes, by which the numerals were increased to ninteen, and beyond which the numeral system of the Runes does not extend.

The 3 double-runes are,

ᛮ al, Arlaugr. 17.
ᛯ mm, Tvimadr. 18.
ᛰ tt, Belgthor. 19.

To express the subsequent numbers, several Runes were combined.

ᛅᛅ (= twice ten) denoted 20. ᛅᛅᚠ = 21. ᛅᛅᚢ = 22 and so on.

RUNES

compared with the Gothic Alphabet of Ulfilas.

Northern Runes			Golden Bracteates	Golden Horn		Anglo-Saxon			Alphabet of Ulfilas		
ᚠ	fé	f	ᚠ	ᚠ		ᚠ	feoh	f	Ⅎ	faíhu	φ
ᚢ	úr	u v	ᚢ			ᚢ ᚪ	ur	u	⊓	urus	ᴕ o
ᚦ	Þurs Þorn	Þ ð	Þ	Þ		Þ	Þorn	Þ	ψ	Þaúrnus	Ϥ
⌿ ⌿	ós	o	ᚱ	ᚠ	a	ᚠ	os	o	ᚦ	ans	α
ᚱ	reið	r	ᚱ	ᚱ	r	ᚱ	rad	r	ᚱ	raiða	ρ
ᚴ	kaun	k g	ᚲ	ᚲ	c (k)	ᚳ ᚻ ᚻ	cen	c (k)	ᚱ	kaunzama	k c (γ x)
			ᚷ	ᚷ	g	ᚷ	gyfu	g	Γ	giba	γ
			ᚹ	ᚹ	v	ᚹ	wen	w	ᛃ ᛈ	vinja	v ʋ
✳ᚺᚺ	hagal	h	ᚺ	ᚺᚺ	h	ᚻᚾ ⌿	hægl	h	· ʜ	hagls	h
ᛏ ᛏ	nauð	n	ᛏ	ᛏ	n	ᛏ	nyd	n	ᚻ	náuþs	ν
ᛁ	is	i	ᛁ	ᛁ	i	ᛁ	is	i	ᛁ	eis	ι (η υ ε ει)
ᛏ ᛁ	ár	a	ᛩ			φ φ	ger	ge (-y)	G	jér	ι
(⋏)	(ŷr)		ᛊ			ᛈ ᛚ	coh	eo	z z	iuja	ζ (σ)
			ᛒ			ᚻ	peorð	p	Π	paírþr	π
			Ψ			Ⱶ	eolhx				
ᚺ	sól	s	ᛊ	ᛉ	s	ᚺ	sigel	s	s Ɛ Ⅼ	sójil	σ (ζ)
ᛏ ᛏ	týr	t d	ᛏ	ᛏ	t	ᛏ	tir	t	ᛐ	tius	τ
ᛒ	biarkan	b p	ᛒ	ᛒ		ᛒ	beorc	b	ʙ ʙ	baírika	β (v)
			ᛗ	ᛗ	e	ᛗ	eh	e	⍬ (~)	aíhvus	η (ιεαιαε)
ᛉ Ⴔ	maðr	m	ᛗ	ᛦ	m	ᛗ ᛘ	man	m	ᚻ	manna	μ
ᚱ	lögr	l	ᚱ	ᚱ	l	ᚱ	lagu	l	ᛚ	lagus	λ
			◇	◇	gg (ng)	ᛜ	ing	ng	X ✕	iggvs	χ (k)
			ᛪ	ᛗ	d	ᚻ	dæg	d	ᛞ	dags	δ (Ϥ)
			(ᚻ)	ᛪ	o	ᛇ	eðel	ð œ	℺	óþal	ω (o ou)
						ᚾ	ac	á			
						ᚠ	æsc	æ			
						ᛠ	yr	y			
						ᚥ	ear	ea			
						✳	ior	io			
						Ψ ⍙	calc				
						⋈⋈	stan	st			
						⋇⋇	gar	g